Hawai'i

HAWAI'I BY ROAD

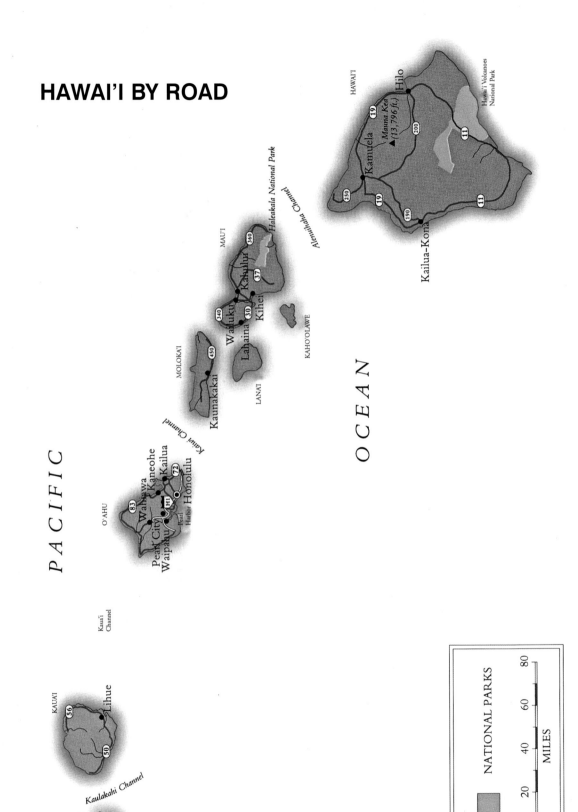

HAWAI'I

Hilo

Mauna Kea
(13,796 ft.)

Hawai'i Volcanoes
National Park

19

200

111

Kamuela

250

19

130

111

Kailua-Kona

Haleakala National Park

MAUI

360

Kahului

37

Wailuku

Lahaina

30

Kihei

340

KAHOOLAWE

Atenuihaha Channel

MOLOKAI

Kaunakakai

450

LANAI

Pailolo Channel

O C E A N

O'AHU

Wahiawa

Kaneohe

Kailua

72

Pearl City

Waipahu

Honolulu

Pearl
Harbor

H1

83

Kalui Channel

P A C I F I C

Kaua'i
Channel

KAUAI

Lihue

56

50

Kaulakahi Channel

NIIHAU

NATIONAL PARKS

MILES

0   20   40   60   80

Celebrate the States

Hawai'i

Jake Goldberg and Joyce Hart

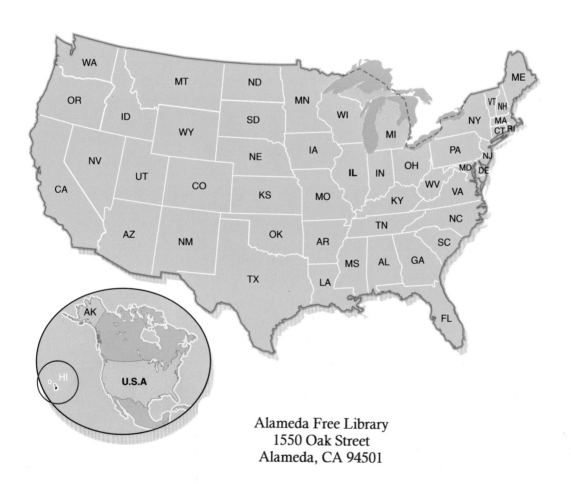

Alameda Free Library
1550 Oak Street
Alameda, CA 94501

Marshall Cavendish
Benchmark
New York

Marshall Cavendish Benchmark
99 White Plains Road
Tarrytown, NY 10591-9001
www.marshallcavendish.us

All Internet addresses were correct and accurate at the time of printing.

Library of Congress Cataloging-in-Publication Data
Goldberg, Jake, 1943–
Hawai'i / by Jake Goldberg and Joyce Hart.—2nd ed.
p. cm. — (Celebrate the states)
Summary: "Provides comprehensive information on the geography, history, wildlife, governmental structure, economy, cultural diversity, peoples, religions, and landmarks of Hawai'i"—Provided by publisher.
Includes bibliographical references and index.
ISBN-13: 978-0-7614-2349-2
ISBN-10: 0-7614-2349-4
1. Hawai'i—Juvenile literature. [1. Hawai'i] I. Hart, Joyce, 1954– II. Title. III. Series.
DU623.25.G644 2007
996.9—dc22
2006010119

Editor: Christine Florie
Editorial Director: Michelle Bisson
Art Director: Anahid Hamparian
Series Designer: Adam Meitlowski

Photo research by Connie Gardner

Cover Photo: Heath Robbins/Taxi/Getty Images

The photographs in this book are used by permission and courtesy of; *Corbis:* Dallas and John Heaton/Free Agents Limited, back cover; Gavriel Jecan, 10; Jim Sugar, 11; Galen Rowell, 15; Michael T. Sedam, 18; Sean Daveys, 21; Mark A. Johnson, 22; Catherine Karnow, 23; Darrell Galin, 25; Bob Krist, 30; Historical Picture Archive, 32; Mike Zens, 34; Bettmann, 37, 43; Hulton Deutsch, 47; David G. Houser, 63; Nik Wheeler, 67; Ronnie Kaufman, 71; Douglas Peebles, 74, 81, 94, 100; Pete Saloutos/zefa, 88; Michael S. Yamashita, 90; David Muench, 103; Dave Bartruff, 106; Bill Ross, 109 (bottom); Gary Braasch, 113; Macduff Everton, 117; Brooks Kraft, 125; Steve Sands, 129; David Sailors, 133; Pat O'Hara, 137. *SuperStock:* Carmel Studios, 8; Steve Vidler, 69; Ron Dahlquist, 72, 105; Roger Allyn Lee, 86; Stock Trek, 89; Tom Brakefield, 93; Alvis Upitis, 96; age fotostock, 98. *Dembinsky Photo Associates:* Phil Degginger, 13; Howard L. Garret, 20; J.S. Sroka, 59. *AP Photo:* Stephen Bortano, 53. *Getty:* Ken Lucas, 29; China Photo, 76. *Granger:* 33, 35, 39, 49, 127. *The Image Works:* Joe Carini, 54, 58; David R. Frazier, 78; Hideo Haga, 121; NASA, 130. *Alamy:* Douglas Peebles, 64; Cornforth Images, 109 (top). *PhotoEdit:* A. Ramey, 70.

Printed in China
1 3 5 6 4 2

Contents

Hawai'i Is . . .

Hawai'i is a place of rare beauty.

"The loveliest fleet of islands that lies anchored to any ocean."
—American writer Mark Twain

"If anyone desires such old-fashioned things as lovely scenery, quiet, pure air, clear sea water, good food and heavenly sunsets . . . I recommend him cordially to [Waikiki Beach]."
—English writer Robert Louis Stevenson

Hawai'i is a place that lingers in people's memories.

"Hawai'i is not a state of mind but a state of grace."
—American author Paul Theroux

"I grew up in Hawai'i, and no matter where I go, Hawai'i will always be my home."
—pianist, composer, teacher Renee Hart

"Although I have spent only short periods of time in Hawai'i over the years, I always compare every other place that I go to with my memories of the islands."
—teacher, basketball coach Brad Lewis

Hawai'i is a place with a troubled past.

"It is our imperative duty to hold these islands with the invincible strength of the American nation."
—U.S. minister to Hawai'i John L. Stevens

"The people of the islands have no voice in determining their future, but are virtually relegated to the condition of the aborigines of the American Continent. An alien element composed of men of energy and determination controls all the resources of Honolulu and will employ them tirelessly to secure their ends."
—Queen Liliuokalani

Hawai'i is a place with a bright and unique future among the fifty states.

"Being Hawai'ian today is finally feeling at home after nearly a century of trying to live like foreigners told us we should live in our own land."
—community leader Abby Napeahi

"The Congress apologizes to Native Hawai'ians on behalf of the people of the United States for the overthrow of the Kingdom of Hawai'i on January 17, 1893 . . . and the deprivation of the rights of Native Hawai'ians to self-determination."
—United States Public Law 103-150, as signed by President Bill Clinton on November 23, 1993

"Hawai'i is unique in its combination of beauty in the natural physical environment, in its people and their Aloha spirit, and in its cosmopolitan mixing of ethnic groups, cultures, religions, and lifestyles. These facets of beauty are to be preserved and enhanced, not only because they are the basis of attraction to visitors but because they are the basis for Hawai'i's attraction to its own people."
—State of Hawai'i Tourism Policy Act

In many ways Hawai'i is a place of tropical beauty, warm weather, and the friendly faces of a multiethnic population. Hawai'i is, in other words, a place that many people dream of escaping to. The astonishing thing about this dream is that a lot of it is true. There are warm beaches to lounge on, a clear-watered ocean that willingly gives up its bounty, and local residents who believe in the aloha spirit—an offering of welcome. But there are also challenges on the islands, just as in any other state in the United States. As the story of Hawai'i unfolds, so, too, do the dreams not only of those who live there but also of those who visit this tropical wonderland.

Note: this book will be using traditional Hawai'ian spelling.

Chapter One

The Island State

The state of Hawai'i rises in the middle of the Pacific Ocean, almost midway between Asia and North America. It sits more than 2,000 miles away from the mainland of the United States, the nation of which it is a part. Hawai'i is an archipelago, or a chain of islands, that stretches in a crescent shape across more than 1,500 miles of ocean, from the island of Hawai'i (called the Big Island), in the southeast, to the tiny island of Kure, in the northwest.

BORN OF FIRE

The Hawai'ian Islands began forming tens of millions of years ago by volcanic eruptions over what today scientists call a hot spot on the floor of the ocean. Hot, molten lava continues to flow from deep within the earth through many of these hot spots.

Solidified by the cool ocean waters, the lava flows formed immense underwater mountains. Over time, as the lava continued to bubble up out of the cone, these underwater mountains grew until they had risen above the ocean surface and became dry land. This land is the Hawai'ian Islands, the largest of all the Pacific island chains.

The Hawai'ian Islands are a group of nineteen islands that are part of an underwater mountain chain.

When molten lava meets the sea, it cools and hardens forming new land.

The volcanoes on the northern islands are dormant (inactive for now) or extinct (they will never erupt again). But three volcanoes on the island of Hawai'i—Mauna Loa, Kilauea, and Hualalai—are active. Mauna Loa has erupted fifteen times since 1900. Kilauea is still pouring out flows of lava to create new land. Haleakala, on the island of Mau'i, is also active.

To the south of the island of Hawai'i a new island is forming. Though it is still about 3,000 feet below the surface of the ocean and not expected to emerge from the sea for ten thousand years, Hawai'ians have already given it a name, Loihi.

LAND OF VOLCANOES

Hawai'i's volcanoes rarely erupt explosively, the way other volcanoes, such as Mount Saint Helens in Washington State or El Chichón in Mexico do. Instead, when heat and pressure build up deep inside the earth under the Hawai'ian volcanoes, hot lava pours freely down the sides of the volcanic cone, building up the cone's height and size, but not shooting large amounts of lava or gases high into the air. Sometimes the lava flows all the way down the mountainsides and slides into the ocean, where it cools. This hardened lava then forms new land.

Kilauea (below) on the island of Hawai'i has been erupting continuously since 1983. Today, on average, Kilauea releases 130,000 gallons of molten lava every minute and has added about 560 acres of new land to Hawai'i. This makes Hawai'i the only state to be adding land.

Kilauea's lava usually flows slowly down its slopes, giving people time to escape its path. In modern times, only one person has been killed (since 1924), but the molten rock, which reaches 2,200 degrees Fahrenheit, has destroyed nearly two hundred homes and has buried an ancient temple and several historic sites. It should be noted that historic accounts of warriors being caught off guard and overcome by lava flows were told in the eighteenth century.

LAND AND WATER

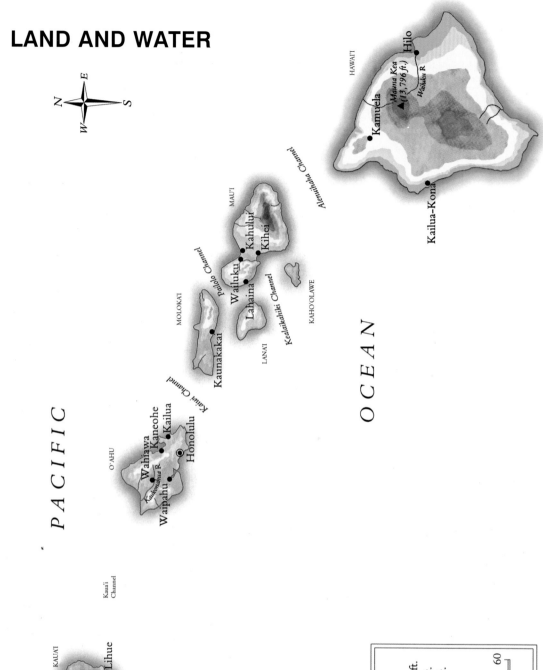

N E
W S

PACIFIC

OCEAN

KAUA'I
Lihue
Waimea R.

NI'IHAU

Kaulakahi Channel

Kaua'i
Channel

Kaua'i Channel

O'AHU
Wahiawa
Kaneohe
Kailua
Waipahu
Kaukonahua R.
Honolulu

MOLOKA'I
Kaunakakai

Pailolo Channel

MAU'I
Kahului
Wailuku
Kihei
Lahaina
LANA'I
Kealaikahiki Channel
KAHO'OLAWE

Alenuihaha Channel

HAWAI'I
Hilo
Kamuela
Mauna Kea
▲ (13,796 ft.)
Waiuku R.
Kailua-Kona

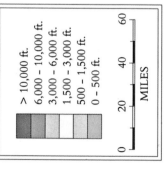

> 10,000 ft.
6,000 – 10,000 ft.
3,000 – 6,000 ft.
1,500 – 3,000 ft.
500 – 1,500 ft.
0 – 500 ft.

0   20   40   60
MILES

EIGHT ISLANDS

There are 137 islands, reefs, and shoals in the Hawai'ian archipelago, but only 8 are considered of major importance. Those are the islands of Hawai'i, Mau'i, Kaho'olawe, Lana'i, Moloka'i, O'ahu, Kaua'i, and Ni'ihau.

Hawai'i

With an area of more than 4,000 square miles, the island of Hawai'i is known locally as the Big Island. The peaks of its two largest volcanoes—Mauna Kea, at 13,796 feet, and Mauna Loa, at 13,679 feet—are high enough to experience snow in winter. Due to its height and the fact that it is situated in the middle of the Pacific Ocean with very little air or light pollution from big cities, Mauna Kea is an excellent place to view the stars. The skies are so clear and the air so pure on top of Mauna Kea that astronomers regard the summit of the volcano as one of the best places on earth to observe the heavens. Today there are thirteen working telescopes near its summit.

Telescopes are located on the summit of Mauna Kea, one of the best locations for ground-based observations of the night sky.

Hilo is the Big Island's largest city, second in size only to the city of Honolulu on the island of O'ahu. Hilo has a small airport and a small port through which travelers, as well as goods, make their entry to the island. In 1960 over five hundred homes and sixty-one people were lost when a large tsunami hit Hilo Bay. Although warnings are occasionally issued, no other major tsunami has hit the island since.

The island of Hawai'i is not noted for sandy beaches. The soil of the island is still very young in geologic time, so most of the rocky coastline has not been worn down into fine particles. There are a few sandy beaches, but they cannot compare with those on the other islands. The Big Island's most famous sandy beach, at one time, was a black sand beach located in Kalapana. Unfortunately, one of Kilauea's eruptions has buried the black sand under several feet of lava. However, near Ka Lae, on the southern tip of the island, there is another small but unique beach that boasts of green sand. It is called the Green Sand Beach. This peculiar sand was created when a lava flow released a large vein of the mineral olivine,

FIVE VOLCANOES

Although Kilauea is the volcano that most people think about when the Big Island is mentioned, five volcanoes actually make up the island. Close to the northern tip of the island are the Kohala Mountains, which include the extinct volcano Kohala. There are also the twin peaks of dormant volcanoes Mauna Kea and Mauna Loa, with a smaller sister volcano slightly to the west called Hualalai. The fifth and most active volcano, Kilauea, is in the southeastern part of the island.

a magnesium-iron silicate that has a glossy luster. Wave action has since pulverized the mineral, creating a uniquely colored sand.

Mau'i

To the northeast of the Big Island lies Mau'i. At over 700 square miles, it is the second-largest island in the Hawai'ian archipelago. Mau'i is shaped somewhat like an hourglass. The northwestern lobe of the island is dominated by the volcano Pu'u Kukui; the southeastern lobe by Haleakala, Mau'i's highest point at over 10,000 feet and the largest dormant volcano in the world.

The central valley that connects the two lobes and gives Mau'i its nickname, the Valley Island, is the island's residential and business center. Sugarcane, pineapple, and other crops are grown there.

The region of Mau'i located between its two volcanoes is a land rich with fertile soil.

The main cities on Mau'i are Kahului, Wailuku, and Lahaina. Industry on Mau'i includes commercial sugar processing and pineapple farming, but the major industry is tourism. Mau'i boasts of having the most beaches (eighty-one) of all the islands. The island is older than the Big Island, and thus its shorelines are more prone to being covered with sand rather than rocks or lava.

One of the biggest attractions associated with Mau'i is its whales, competing with its glorious beaches. Humpback whales, which once were hunted to near extinction from Lahaina, are now protected and studied by conservationists and researches on Mau'i. The whales' song is one focus of the research. People who visit Mau'i have the chance to ride in boats to see up close the migrating whales and to hear the whales' singing as they spend the winter months off the shores of Mau'i.

Although whale watching has become a popular tourist attraction, concern about the safety of the whales has been expressed widely. In the first three months of 2006, five whales were injured when boats accidentally collided with them. The number of such collisions has risen over the years. To help protect the whales, officials have limited the number of boats that offer whale-watching tours.

Kaho'olawe

The tiny island of Kaho'olawe lies south of Mau'i. The smallest of the eight major Hawai'ian Islands, it is currently uninhabited. There are signs, however, that the entire island was at one time fully populated. There are less than 30,000 acres on this small piece of land, but it has a big history. In ancient times it might have played an important role as a training site for early Hawai'ian navigators as they observed the rotation of the stars and studied the ocean currents from vantage points on the small island. In the 1800s it was used as a penal colony and as pastureland for grazing sheep and goats. The animals over-grazed, eating all the ground cover and causing massive soil erosion.

At the start of World War II, in 1941, the U.S. Navy took control of the small island and used it for target practice. A long protest after the war by Hawai'ians demanding that the navy clean up the unexploded bombs and return the island to the state finally was successful. In 1993 the navy turned over control of the island to the State of Hawai'i. Today, Kaho'olawe is a Hawai'ian reserve, set aside for the study and practice of Hawai'ian culture, and is in the process of being restored. It remains uninhabited.

Lana'i

Fewer than three thousand people live on the small island of Lana'i. Its highest point is Lana'ihale, a 3,370-foot-high mountain on the eastern coast. The main town, Lana'i City, is located in the center of the island. Lana'i is sometimes called the Pineapple Island. It was there, in 1922, that James D. Dole established his 15,000-acre pineapple plantation, expanding his canning empire.

Lana'i is only 18 miles wide and 13 miles long. Today, the economy of Lana'i is in the middle of a rapid transition from pineapple production to tourism. Like its neighbor, Moloka'i, the people of Lana'i are advertising the island as a haven for a simpler, uncrowded way of living and vacationing. Most conveniences of the mainland (the other forty-nine states) such as malls and, until not too long ago, taxis were nowhere to be seen. This is changing though, as Lana'i is quickly becoming known as a great hideaway for the rich and famous. New luxury hotels were built in the late 1990s, and the small island airport that once was big enough for propeller planes only has been expanded to handle jets. People who visit Lana'i are happily impressed with snorkeling in the clearest offshore waters of all the other islands.

Moloka'i

To the north of Lana'i and the northwest of Mau'i lies the island of Moloka'i, home to the world's tallest sea cliffs and Kahiwa Falls, the state's tallest waterfall.

For a long time Moloka'i was known as the Lonely Island. People were afraid to visit there because of the leper colony that had been established on the Kalaupapa Peninsula in 1855. Leprosy causes scales and sores on the skin and deforms body parts. Because the disease is infectious, lepers were forced to live apart from everyone else. Modern medicine has done much to control leprosy, and the government began phasing out the leper colony on Moloka'i in 1957, though some patients still live there.

Moloka'i's northern sea cliffs are the tallest in the world, rising 2,000 feet above the sea.

MAU'I NUI

Scientists have found evidence that, about 1.2 million years ago, the islands of Mau'i, Lana'i, Moloka'i, and Kahoolawe were one landmass, bigger by almost 40 percent than the present-day Big Island. As the volcanoes that created this land mass quieted down and became dormant, the lowlands between the volcanoes eventually sank under the ocean. Scientists refer to this ancient landmass as Mau'i Nui, or Big Mau'i.

Today Moloka'i is often called the Friendly Isle, possibly due to the fact that the largest population of Native Hawai'ians live there. Historically, Moloka'i has been a place for the spiritual leaders of the Hawai'ian culture to gather.

Like Lana'i, Moloka'i draws fewer tourists than the other islands do. The land and the people of Moloka'i are probably the least affected by the changes that the other islands are experiencing. Much of the land remains the same as it always has been, with very little commercial development and a great deal of its natural beauty undisturbed.

O'ahu

To the west of Moloka'i lies O'ahu. Though it covers only about 600 square miles, making it the third largest island of the Hawai'ian chain, O'ahu is the most heavily populated of all the islands. Some 899,000 people live there, amounting to about 70 percent of the state's population. The island of O'ahu is dominated by two mountain ranges, the Waianae range along the western coast and the Koolau Mountains to the east.

In the southeastern corner of the island is the city of Honolulu, the state capital. Honolulu is also the state's principal port, the site of its major international airport, and its business and financial center. To the west is Pearl Harbor, the site of the American naval base bombed by the Japanese, provoking the United States to enter World War II.

I'olani Palace, the only seat of former royalty in the United States, is situated in downtown Honolulu. This is where the last queen of the islands lived before the United States overthrew the Hawai'ian monarchy in 1893. As Hawai'i's urban center, Honolulu is also home to many other historic buildings, art galleries, museums, ukulele shops, aquariums, and, of course, restaurants and hotels, which fill up the city landscape. There is also a Chinatown in the southwest corner of Honolulu, where several Asian cultures can be explored in various communities, shops, and restaurants.

Honolulu is a bustling city and the largest in Hawai'i.

During winter months, O'ahu experiences some of the biggest waves in the world.

On the southern side of the city is Waikiki Beach, Hawai'i's most famous beach, where millions of tourists from around the world lounge in the sun each year. At the end of Waikiki Beach is the equally famous Diamond Head, an extinct volcanic crater.

Despite O'ahu's large population, once visitors get away from the city limits of Honolulu, they can still find unspoiled rain forests, waterfalls, and beautiful sandy beaches. The sport of surfing originated in the Hawai'ian Islands, and O'ahu has some of the best surfing beaches in the world. Competitive surfers rush to O'ahu's northern shore beaches, especially in the winter when storms cause heavy surging. At times like that, beaches such as Banzai Pipeline often are pummeled by waves 20 feet tall or higher.

DIAMOND HEAD

Diamond Head's Hawai'ian name is *Laeahi*, which means "brow of the tuna." This name was given because when you look at the crater from the side, it resembles the silhouette of a large tuna (or ahi), one of the staples of the Hawai'ian diet. In the 1880s, however, Diamond Head was named by British soldiers who were not thinking of the sea. When they first saw the crater, they noticed something reflecting light off the sides of this massive volcanic form. They thought they had discovered diamonds. The shiny stones, however, turned out to be calcite crystals, a common crystal often found in limestone seashells.

Kaua'i

Kaua'i is the most northern of the main islands and is fourth in size. It is the oldest island, therefore, it has the deepest soil. Time and weather have worn down the basic volcanic foundation into very fertile soil so plants thrive. This is why Kaua'i is known as the Garden Island and is often thought to be the most beautiful of all the Hawai'ian Islands.

The entire island of Kaua'i was formed from the single eruption of a large volcano. Two peaks of this volcano dominate the landscape, with Kawaikini being the higher at 5,243 feet. The other peak, Wai 'ale' ale, only 100 feet shorter, holds the world's record as the wettest place on earth, averaging almost 500 inches of rain a year. Wrapped in clouds much of the time, the mountains are covered with lush vegetation.

The island's rugged, mountainous interior has steep valleys and gorges. The most spectacular valley in all the islands is located on Kaua'i. It is Waimea Canyon and is located on the western side of the island. Ten miles long, a mile wide, and a half-mile deep, Waimea has been called the Grand Canyon of the Pacific. The mountains are surrounded by white sandy beaches (almost 90 miles of them) along the coast.

Lihue is the biggest city on Kaua'i and is located on the southeastern corner of the island. Kaua'i's ports, both air and water, are found at Lihue.

Rivers and floodwaters carved the Waimea Canyon thousands of years ago.

Kaua'i was the site of the first commercial sugar plantations in the islands and is less involved in the tourism business than O'ahu, Mau'i, and the Big Island. In 1983 and 1992 Kaua'i took the brunt of two huge hurricanes, which destroyed several hotels and frightened tourists away for some years.

Ni'ihau

The tiny island of Ni'ihau lies 17 miles west of Kaua'i. Its 72 square miles are privately owned. Today it is home to fewer than three hundred people, mostly cattle ranchers and farmers. Ni'ihau is important, though, because it has the largest concentration of pure-blooded Native Hawai'ians in the entire state. Hawai'ian is still taught in the schools of Ni'ihau as the primary language.

SUNSHINE AND RAIN

Hawai'i's climate is warm and tropical. There is little difference in the weather between summer and winter. Throughout the year, temperatures in the lowlands are in the seventies and eighties during the day and drop to the sixties at night. The coldest temperature ever recorded was on top of Mauna Kea on the Big Island, when the thermometer dipped down to 12 degrees Fahrenheit in 1979. The hottest temperature, 100 °F, occurred in 1931, in Puna (not far from Kilauea volcano) on the Big Island. Water temperatures around the shores of the islands are usually about 73 °F in the winter and 80 °F in the summer.

Most of the time steady northeasterly trade winds blow moisture from the Pacific Ocean across the islands. The air condenses its water vapor on the slopes of Hawai'i's volcanic peaks and mountain ranges. The result is warm, wet weather on the northeastern, or windward, side of the islands and hot, dry weather on the western, or leeward, side for most of the year.

That accounts for the island's astonishing geographical contrasts between dense, wet rain forests on one side and dry, somewhat desertlike terrain on the other. Hawai'i does occasionally experience hurricanes, thunderstorms, flash floods, earthquakes, and tsunamis. Rainfall averages range from about 6 inches annually in Puako on the dry side of the Big Island to almost 500 inches on the slopes of Mount Wai'ali 'ali on Kaua'i. Rainfall in Hawai'i seldom covers a whole island. If it is raining on one side, you most often can travel to the other side and still enjoy the sunshine.

A COLORFUL WORLD

Throughout Hawai'i, flowers and trees bloom in a rainbow of colors, making the islands seem like a lush paradise. Yellow hibiscus, the state flower, is a tropical shrub that flourishes over all the islands. Another common plant is bougainvillea, with blooms of bright purple, magenta, pink, and white. There are also yellow ginger, red anthurium, orange trumpet vine, and many colors of wild orchids. Pikake is a variety of jasmine that is often used in lei, the wreath of flowers that are draped around the necks of people on special occasions. The fragrant frangipani is also frequently used to make lei, as is the sweet-smelling plumeria flower. Profusions of brightly colored flowers adorn streets and homes and public places and fill the air with their fragrant scent.

A flower garden blooms with color on Mau'i.

Many of the tropical trees that grow in Hawai'i's luxuriant forests also produce beautiful flowers. The jacaranda has brilliant violet blossoms. The African tulip tree produces bright red flowers. The ohia, which also blooms in red, was thought to be a favorite of Pele, the fire goddess, and was considered sacred by the original Hawai'ians. Equally brilliant are the flowers of the bauhinia and the wiliwili, or Australian umbrella tree. The royal poinciana was brought from Madagascar and produces bright scarlet blossoms, while the shower tree blooms in pink, coral, gold, and multicolored shades.

Some tropical trees also have practical and traditional uses. The woods of the hau and the milo are used for making canoes and bowls. The leaves of the pandanus and ti trees are used to weave mats and clothing. Tropical fruit trees furnish bananas, coconuts, lychee, macadamia nuts, papayas, guavas, and mangoes. At Kona, on the island of Hawai'i, commercial coffee bean plantations are found.

PROTECTING THE UNIQUE

For millions of years the Hawai'ian Islands were barren of all life. Strong Pacific winds, heavy tropical rains, and powerful ocean currents eroded the huge masses of lava, carving deep, razor-sharp valleys and high coastal cliffs out of the gently sloping mountains. In some parts of Hawai'i, such a volcanic landscape remains stark and sterile, so much so that in the 1960s the Apollo astronauts were sent to the dormant volcano of Haleakala on Mau'i to train for walking on the moon.

But as time passed and lava was broken down into soil, most of the Hawai'ian Islands were transformed into a lush paradise of exotic plants and animals. Seeds were carried there by the wind and by seabirds, and insects probably arrived on floating driftwood. In the warm and wet climate, these plants and animals flourished and multiplied until the raw, lifeless, gray-and-black volcanic landscape was covered with thick vegetation in a thousand shades of green. Because of its geographical isolation, more than 90 percent of the plants and animals native to Hawai'i are found nowhere else in the world.

For many centuries no humans disturbed idyllic Hawai'i. But with the arrival of the Polynesians, followed by the Europeans, Asians, and Americans, the islands' unique ecosystem was changed forever. Today, many indigenous Hawai'ian species are extinct or are near extinction because they cannot compete with those introduced by humans. Because of that, some people refer to the Hawai'ian Islands as the Endangered Species Capital of the World. Of all the plants and animals listed in the United States as being endangered, almost one-third of them are found only in Hawai'i. Pigs, goats, and cats, brought by settlers and allowed to roam wild, have killed off many native species. The once domesticated pigs and goats rove through the forests, eating and trampling delicate plants. Hawai'ian birds had no natural predators, so they often nested on the ground. That made them easy prey when invaders arrived. Years ago, sugar-plantation owners imported small, ferretlike animals called mongooses to control their rat problem. The mongooses ate bird's eggs instead of rats. Today, only the island of Kaua'i, where the mongooses never became established, still has large populations of many species of native birds. In Kaua'i's rain forests rare creatures such as the 'a'o bird still live, but they no longer are found on the other islands.

Insects and snakes that arrive on planes and boats also do much damage to Hawai'i's fragile environment. Some insects infest and kill plants. Others carry diseases that are fatal to birds. Still others eat the larvae of the bees and flies that are necessary to pollinate plants. Even plants that settlers have brought in—from ornamental trees to blackberry bushes—can quickly crowd out the original species.

This invasion of foreign plants and animals has been catastrophic. The koloa, or Hawai'ian duck, and the nene, or Hawai'ian goose, are both endangered. The monk seal is seen only in remote areas of the islands, far from people. Half of Hawai'i's bird species are now extinct. Hawai'i is home to 40 percent of the birds and 44 percent of the plants on the endangered species lists for the entire United States. There are more than a hundred species of Hawai'ian plants that have fewer than twenty individual specimens still clinging to life.

Hawai'ian residents and visitors are now keenly aware of the need to protect the remaining native species. Some are preserved in special areas such as the Leeward Islands, a group of about a dozen tiny islands northwest of Ni'ihau. Special permission is required to visit most of these islands as they are part of the Hawai'ian Islands National Wildlife Refuge and are sanctuaries to millions of seabirds and other endangered species such as the monk seal. Laysan Island, one of the Leewards, has the world's largest colony of albatrosses, though there used to be many more. In the last decade of the nineteenth century, it was discovered that the albumin found in albatross eggs could be used in making an ingredient needed in developing photographic film, and "egg sweeping" parties greatly reduced the number of birds on the island.

Conservationists are trying to find ways to stem the tide of foreign species that enter on planes. Many of these creatures come from Guam. At the airport there, dogs sniff the cargo areas of planes, searching for snakes and other animal stowaways.

On Mau'i, public and private landowners have cooperated to protect 100,000 acres of forest on the north slope of Haleakala Crater. Under this program fences have been erected around the most delicate sections of Haleakala to keep out the hungry feral pigs and goats. Hunting of these animals is also allowed. But park rangers still have to keep a vigilant eye out for other non-native species of plants and insects that are always creeping in.

In the future such cooperation between public and private interests will be even more necessary to protect Hawai'i's unique environment so that locals and tourists alike may continue to enjoy its rare and delicate beauty.

THE HAWAI'IAN MONK SEAL

Found nowhere else in the world, the Hawai'ian monk seal is more than fifteen million years old—the oldest of all seals. There are two other species of monk seals, but only a few hundred Mediterranean monk seals remain and the Caribbean variety is already extinct. In the nineteenth century explorers and seamen nearly killed off the Hawai'ian species as well. Today there are about 1,400 monk seals left in the Hawai'ian Islands. Most of them live on the small sandy islands in the northern part of the archipelago, but a few are still seen on the main islands. In 1997 a rare event was recorded when the first known monk seal pup was born on the island of Mau'i.

Although nobody hunts these animals anymore, humans can still hurt them. The leading cause of death for monk seals is getting tangled up in fishnets, which prevents them from reaching the surface of the water to breathe. Humans causing disturbances can also lead to the death of young pups. Hungry sharks are another danger.

Chapter Two

The Past

The story of America's fiftieth state is rich in individual tales of uprooted peoples journeying to a strange new home; of striving to get along with people of many different backgrounds; of hard, tedious, and dangerous years of labor at low wages; and of heroic efforts to create a better life.

THE FIRST HAWAI'IANS

While the Hawai'ian Islands were still unpopulated, in the years preceding 300 C.E., events that would change the islands forever were taking place thousands of miles to the west, on the continent of Asia. Overpopulation and hostility from other tribes caused peoples from what are now India, Myanmar, Thailand, and other areas to move to the tip of the Malaysian Peninsula. Over time they intermarried. Eventually they undertook the daunting adventure of sailing out into the waters that surrounded them and populated the thousands of Pacific islands now referred to as Indonesia.

There, they became expert fishermen and sailors and learned how to build large, oceangoing dugout canoes that they used to travel from island to island. As they became ever more daring navigators, these people

A tiki sculpture is carved in the shape of a Polynesian god.

Masked rowers paddle among the islands of the Pacific.

continued to migrate eastward into the region of the South Pacific now known as Polynesia, which means "many islands."

About two thousand years ago sailors from the Marquesas Islands in Polynesia set out across the vast ocean in search of new lands even farther away. They sailed north across 2,000 miles of open water, at a time when most European seamen were afraid to venture out of sight of land. Even today, the boldness of these early Polynesian journeys astounds historians. "It was left to the men of the Pacific," wrote historical novelist James Michener, "to meet an ocean on its own terms and to conquer it. Lacking both metals and maps, sailing with only the stars . . . these men accomplished miracles."

After long and perilous voyages, these Polynesian sailors came to a large, lush, inviting island. They believed that they had rediscovered the mythical paradise, which they had been told about in stories, from which their people had originated. So they named the island Hawai'i, the name it was called in their ancient legends. The new inhabitants arrived in two waves, one around 500 C.E. and a second around 1200.

Monarchs and chiefs, or *alii*, who were believed to be descended from the gods, ruled over the common people with the help of their priests, or kahunas. The kahunas were responsible for passing on the Hawai'ian mythology, or stories about their gods, and the tales of their Polynesian past. Kahunas also maintained social order through a system of castes and *kapus*.

Social castes designated what each person was responsible for or what tasks they had to do in order to maintain their tribe. If a boy's father belonged to the warrior caste, for instance, that boy would grow up to be a soldier. Likewise, a person could not become a monarch unless he or she was born into the family of monarchs. Only royalty could own land. People not of the royal caste were allowed to use the land but could not own it. This system helped the kahunas to manage the community.

Hawai'i had a warrior society. Warriors were referred to as koa, a name given to them from the name of the hard wood tree their weapons were made from.

The kapu system (which was a set of rules that told the people what they could not do) was often oppressive. For example, anyone who was not related to the leaders of the tribe could not come too close to the chiefs, walk in their footsteps, touch their possessions, or cast a shadow on their property. The kapus were taken very seriously for several reasons. One was that the people believed their chiefs and kahunas were sacred people with divine knowledge. The other reason was that the penalty for violation of these rules was usually death.

A PLACE OF REFUGE

Throughout the islands there were once places of refuge called *pu'uhonua* in Hawai'ian. Some of these were built so that women and children would be safe during times of war. Places of refuge were often hard to get to, thus they offered safety. Others who took advantage of such a place of refuge were soldiers who had been defeated in battle.

Another use of these places of refuge was for anyone who broke a kapu. A person who was found guilty of breaking a kapu was often allowed to escape to a designated sacred refuge, usually located near a Hawaiian *heiau*, or sacred temple. There a kahuna could purify the person who had broken the rules; and that person could then return to his village without fear of punishment. One of these ancient places is preserved at the City of Refuge National Historical Park on the Kona coast of the island of Hawai'i.

The first Hawai'ians lived off the riches of the sea and the cultivation of the land. Those who were great fishers lived near the coastline, while those who had farming skills lived farther up the sides of the mountains or deep in the valleys. The villagers then would trade their goods, swapping fish and seaweed, for example, for sweet potatoes, yams, and taro roots. Other foods in their diet included pork and chicken, which had been brought from Polynesia, as well as bananas, sugarcane, coconuts, bamboo, and breadfruit.

Early Hawai'ians did not have a written language, so there are no written accounts of their early history. Instead, they learned their history from one another through oral traditions—chants and legends—and the hula dance. The integrity of the chants and dances was carefully observed because changing a word or a step would change history. Knowingly changing a chant or hula would result in severe punishment.

As the Polynesians arrived on the various islands in Hawai'i, it is known that tribes were formed. Each island probably had one monarch who ruled over it. At times, either to gain access to more land, more food, or to increase royal power, battles erupted among the tribes.

KING KAMEHAMEHA I

The birth of the child who would one day become the first king of all the Hawai'ian Islands was disturbing to some of the people of that time (probably 1738). It is said that a bright star (possibly Comet Halley) appeared in the sky on the night of Kamehameha's birth, signaling that this little baby boy would grow up to be a fierce warrior, or so the people believed. The infant who was to become King Kamehameha was born on

Kamehameha I was the first king of the Hawai'ian islands.

the Big Island. Some tribal chiefs feared this young baby might one day threaten their power, and the legend goes that they sought to kill him. The future king was therefore raised in hiding under very tight security for the first few years of his life. Later the chiefs would invite the young boy into their courts and train him. As a young man, he already held high rank. By the time Captain Cook arrived in the islands in 1778, Kamehameha was on his way to becoming the first king of a unified Hawai'i.

THE ARRIVAL OF CAPTAIN COOK

In January 1778 two ships, the *Resolution* and the *Discovery*, sailed into Waimea Bay at the island of Kaua'i. The vessels were under the command of Captain James Cook, an Englishman who had been commissioned to explore and map the South Pacific.

Cook named these islands that he had stumbled onto the Sandwich Islands, after the Earl of Sandwich, who had sponsored his voyage. Cook stayed only for two weeks before sailing off, but after ten months he returned, hoping to repair his ships and stock up on more food, freshwater, and supplies.

At first the Hawai'ians marveled at the appearance of these *haoles*, or foreigners, fair-skinned men who wore a strange cloth skin all over their bodies and had supplies of highly prized iron. The British visitors were amazed at the welcome they received from the islanders. "I have nowhere in this sea seen such a number of people assembled in one place," Cook wrote in his journal. "Besides those in the canoes, all the shore of the bay was covered with people, and hundreds were swimming around the ships like shoals of fish." The Hawai'ians held great feasts for the visitors, without expecting anything in return for their hospitality.

The natives of Hawai'i greet Captain Cook upon his arrival to the islands.

After a time, however, the friendly Hawai'ians grew impatient with Captain Cook's men. The British broke many kapus and stole objects from sacred temples. Though Cook is considered one of the more enlightened explorers, he and his crew killed several Hawai'ians. He also continued to demand that the islanders provide food and supplies for his voyage.

The Hawai'ians had had enough of these pale visitors. Lieutenant James King, one of Cook's crew, commented that the Hawai'ians grew "very inquisitive about our time of departure." John Ledyard, another crewman, confirmed that the British had worn out their welcome. "It was also equally evident from the looks of the natives," Ledyard wrote, that "our former friendship was at an end, and that we had nothing to do but hasten our departure to some different island where our vices were not known."

One day Captain Cook became furious over the theft of one of the *Discovery*'s small boats. He went ashore, planning to kidnap the king and hold him hostage until the boat was returned. As Cook forcibly escorted the king to the beach, the large crowd of Hawai'ians who had gathered grew angry. A fight broke out and Cook was clubbed and stabbed to death. His shocked men sailed away with his remains, and he was buried at sea.

OUTSIDERS RUSH IN

From that time on, ships from England, France, Spain, the United States, and Russia made frequent stops in the Hawai'ian Islands to rest and trade for fresh water, tropical fruits, fresh meat and fish, and such prized commodities as sandalwood, a rare fragrant wood. Hawai'i lay right on the trade route that had sprung up across the Pacific: pelts and furs were sent from Alaska and the Pacific Northwest to China, where they were exchanged for tea, silk, and porcelain. Soon small communities of Europeans—merchants, traders, and farmers—were established on the islands.

Meanwhile, Kamehameha began his conquest of the Big Island. By 1791 the island was securely under his power, and he easily went on to take control of the islands of Mau'i and Moloka'i. Four years later, equipped with guns and ammunition gained from trade with Europeans, Kamehameha set sail for Oa'hu with 1,200 war canoes and ten thousand warriors, determined to bring Oa'hu under his control. After several very bloody battles, Kamehameha and his men were successful. Later, in 1810, fearing the power of Kamehameha, the chiefs of Kaua'i surrendered, and Kamehameha declared himself the first king of all the Hawai'ian Islands.

Kamehameha ruled for nine years. He was a confident diplomat and worked with European countries and the United States to ensure the independence of the Hawai'ian Islands for far longer than most of the other Pacific Islands. He died in 1819. From his deathbed he implored the native islanders to keep their traditions and to "enjoy what I have made right." But his oldest son, Liholiho, known as Kamehameha II, had other ideas. He abolished the elaborate system of kapu, which had made life so difficult for the common people. Though women were not supposed to eat with men in public, one day Liholiho sat down alongside his wife and stepmother at an elaborate feast. With this simple act, the six-hundred-year-old kapu system collapsed and the Hawai'ian traditional culture began to fade.

With the approval of a council of chiefs, King Kamehameha's son, Liholiho, became king on May 21, 1819.

LITTLE MOHEE

Nineteenth-century whalers often sailed south to Mau'i on their homeward voyage after a season of hunting their prey in the frigid Arctic waters. The woman in this song was a native of Mau'i, pronounced "Mohee" by the sailors.

As I went out walk-ing up - on a fine day,

I got aw-ful lone-some as the day passed a - way.

I sat down a - mus - ing a - lone on the grass,

When who should sit by me,_____ But a sweet In-dian lass._____

She sat down beside me upon a fine day.
I got awful lonesome as the day passed away,
She asked me to marry, and gave me her hand,
Said, "My pappy's a chieftain all over this land."

"My pappy's a chieftain and ruler he,
I'm his only daughter and my name is Mohee."
I answered and told her that it never could be,
'Cause I had my own sweetheart in my own country.

I had my own sweetheart and I knew she loved me,
Her heart was as true as any Mohee.
So I said, "I must leave you and goodbye my dear,
There's a wind in my canvas and home I must steer."

At home with relations I tried for to see,
But there wasn't one there like my little Mohee;
And the girl I had trusted proved untrue to me,
So I sailed o'er the ocean to my little Mohee.

Christian missionaries quickly flocked in, building churches and establishing schools in their attempts to convert the Hawai'ians to their religion. By 1831 there were more than 50,000 Hawai'ians studying Western culture in Christian schools. Often the Protestant missionaries taught the Hawai'ians that their ancestors were primitive and sinful pagans. Sometimes the price of a Western education led to the loss of respect for Hawai'ian beliefs. A frequent visitor to the islands, Russian explorer Otto von Kotzebue, found Hawai'i much changed by the missionaries. "The streets, formerly so full of life and animation, are now deserted," Kotzebue wrote. "Games of all kinds, even the most innocent, are sternly prohibited; singing is a punishable offense; and . . . attempting to dance would certainly find no mercy."

KING SUGAR

By the 1840s Western influence was strong throughout the islands. The port cities of Honolulu, Hilo, and Lahaina had become bustling centers of commerce with the freewheeling atmosphere of U.S. frontier towns. Honolulu had six hundred permanent European and American residents, and thousands of sailors from many nations took their shore leaves in the islands.

In 1833 a group of Boston merchants, Ladd & Company, opened a large trading house in Honolulu. One of the firm's partners, William Hooper, purchased land on Kaua'i and began growing sugarcane in 1835. He built a mill to grind the cane stalks and press out their juice. Then the liquid sugar was boiled into molasses and sugar crystals. Hooper's plantation was the beginning of what would become Hawai'i's major industry in the second half of the nineteenth century.

Sugar was Hawai'i's leading agricultural export by the mid-1800s. But the plantation owners faced a serious problem—they could not find enough laborers among the Hawai'ians to grow and harvest the cane. At the time of

Captain Cook's visit, more than 300,000 people lived in Hawai'i. By 1853 the number of Native Hawai'ians had dwindled to around 70,000. Many had died of diseases introduced by the foreigners. Some young men had left the islands, seeking adventure by becoming sailors aboard foreign ships. Many who remained simply refused to work under the harsh conditions found in the cane fields.

The planters solved this problem by bringing in workers from other nations. They looked to Asia for contract workers, people who, in exchange for free passage to Hawai'i, promised to labor in the cane fields for three to five years. They received wages of a few dollars a day, shelter, food, and some medical care. After their contract period was up, they were free to do as they pleased.

At first the planters brought in Chinese workers, then East Indians and Japanese, and then Koreans and Filipinos. Between 1850 and 1920, more than 300,000 immigrants from various parts of Asia arrived to seek their fortunes in the cane fields of Hawai'i.

A group of Chinese farm workers pose by their harvested pineapples.

At the beginning of that period, people of native Hawai'ian heritage made up more than 90 percent of the population of the Hawai'ian Islands. By the end of it, Hawai'ians represented a scant 16 percent of the population and Caucasians less than 8 percent. People of Asian descent made up a great majority of the island's population—62 percent.

During the second half of the nineteenth century, Hawai'ian society was transformed. The traditional Hawai'ian community and its culture were all but gone. But a new, vibrant, multicultural community, one that makes Hawai'i unique among the fifty states even today, was born.

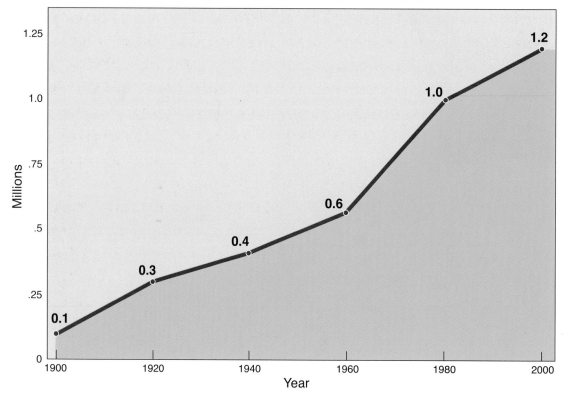

POPULATION GROWTH: 1900–2000

The single greatest force driving this change was King Sugar. In spite of the obvious challenges and hardships, such as the backbreaking work that laborers in the cane fields had to withstand, historian John W. Vandercook chose to describe this era in this way: "the farms where [the workers] lived in close communities of many thousands have turned into towns as racially cosmopolitan as any in the world. It is by no means the least of the sugar industry's accomplishments that in such towns the various groups live amiably together."

FROM KINGDOM TO STATE

Throughout the nineteenth century, the Caucasian—known as haole in Hawai'ian—population was on the rise. Many of them were rich merchants, traders, and plantation owners. Since the taxes of their businesses paid for the Hawai'ian government, they had a powerful influence on the monarchy. Some of these white businessmen became the king's closest advisers.

With exposure to Western ideas of democracy came efforts by Hawai'ians to reform the monarchy and limit its powers. In 1840 Kamehameha II announced a new written constitution that gave many powers to an elected legislature. Traditionally, all the land in the islands was owned by the king and the noble families. Then, in 1848, Kamehameha III initiated the Great Mahele, a land-reform program that permitted individual ownership of private property and granted thousands of acres to commoners.

These reforms did not please all Hawai'ians. The powers of the king had been reduced, but the legislature could be manipulated by the haoles to serve their business interests. Even the land-reform program made it much easier for foreigners to buy and control large tracts of land for sugar and pineapple plantations, removing many options for ordinary islanders.

In 1855 King Kamehameha IV began his rule at the age of twenty and remained in power for only nine years before his untimely death. His legacy was the building of hospitals on Oa'hu and Mau'i to care for ailing Hawai'ians, with a special emphasis on influenza and leprosy. The next king, Kamehameha V, who reigned from 1863 to his death in 1872, is remembered for promoting tourism in the islands. Kamehameha V was a bachelor and died without an heir, thus causing the Kamehameha dynasty to die with him.

There were two major contenders for the monarchy. One was William Charles Lunalilo, cousin of King Kamehameha V. The other was David Kalakaua, who was a descendant of the high chiefs who had helped to raise King Kamehameha I to power. Lunalilo was the more popular candidate by far, as he was known to support the common people. Although it would not count as official, Lunalilo suggested that all the people of Hawai'i should vote for their choice for king. Lunalilo won by a landslide. Since no one had been assigned to the monarchy by King Kamehameha V, the next Hawai'ian king, according to the constitution, was to be appointed by the legislature. After seeing the results of the popular vote, the legislature, in 1873, unanimously appointed Lunalilo to become the next king.

King Lunalilo's two main objectives were to make the Hawai'ian government more democratic and to improve Hawai'i's economy. For democracy, he revised one major change that King Kamehameha V had made. Lunalilo restored the second house in the legislature, the one that was made up of representatives elected by the people. For the economy, King Lunalilo attempted to make a deal with the United States. He would cede Pearl Harbor to the U.S. military in exchange for the right to ship Hawai'ian sugar into the United States without having to pay special taxes. When the Hawai'ian people heard of this, however, they were in great disagreement with the king. This deal did not go through in King Lunalilo's time. His health, already frail, deteriorated, and he died after having been on the throne for only one year. In his place the legislature appointed King Lunalilo's previous opponent, David Kalakaua.

King David Kalakaua, the last reigning king of Hawai'i, is remembered as the Merrie Monarch. He not only enjoyed parties, music, and other forms of entertainment, but he was also very much involved in reviving the Hawai'ian culture, in particular the traditional Hawai'ian chanting and hula. He is referred to as being conservative, but this did not apply to his spending of money. For example, he rebuilt the extremely expensive I'olani Palace, the royal residence and the seat of government. Actually, there was an I'olani Palace already built when he came to power, but King Kalakaua had that one torn down. Then he spent over $350,000 (a very huge sum in those times) to build a new one. The new palace had indoor plumbing (bathrooms and running water), electricity, and telephones, even before the White House had them.

King Kalakaua was the first Hawai'ian king to visit Washington, D.C. While he was there, President Ulysses S. Grant held a state dinner in King Kalakaua's honor. Later the king spoke to the U.S. Congress. He also signed a treaty with the United States to reduce tariffs (taxes on imports or exports) so that goods, especially sugar, could be traded more freely and more cheaply with the United States.

Under King Kalakaua, Native Hawai'ian culture enjoyed a revival until 1887 when the Hawai'ian League overtook the government and enforced a new constitution, restricting his powers.

This promoted a better economy in Hawai'i, as the sugar industry was quickly expanding. The United States, in return, was given the right to use Pearl Harbor, which it later built into a U.S. naval port.

In 1887 a group of wealthy people who had grown tired of King Kalakaua's lavish spending confronted him with guns and forced him to agree to what has become known as the Bayonet Constitution—a revision of Hawai'i's old constitution—which restricted the vote to property owners and stripped away much of the king's power. After the revised constitution went into effect, the legislature could override any of the king's vetoes and the king could not take any actions unless they were first approved by the legislature.

Three years later King Kalakaua's health failed, and he died in 1891. His sister, Lili'uokalani, succeeded him.

A MUSICAL KING

King Kalakaua not only loved to hear music, he was also a musician and a composer. Among the songs he wrote was *Hawai'i Pono'i*, which has become the Hawai'i state anthem. For his promotion of Hawai'ian culture, specifically for his support in bringing back the traditional Hawai'ian hula, a festival has been named in his honor. The Merrie Monarch Festival is held in Hilo, on the Big Island, each year in spring. Contestants from all of the islands and from the mainland travel to the festival to compete in both traditional and modern hula.

Queen Lili'uokalani was determined to restore power to the monarchy and to rid the island of foreign control. To do this, she tried to revise the constitution. The legislature, however, which had gained substantial power with the new constitution, failed to support Lili-uokalani. Two years into her reign, in 1893, a group of businessmen and sugar planters, aided by U.S. troops, stormed the royal palace and overthrew the queen. This was an illegal act, so President Grover Cleveland of the United States sent a representative, James H. Blount, to look into the situation. Blount concluded that Queen Lili'uokalani should be restored to

Queen Lili'uokalani was Hawai'i's last queen.

power. There was one condition, however, and the queen's hesitancy on this issue may have caused her being dethroned.

The U.S. government insisted that Queen Lili'uokalani not hold any criminal charges against the men who had stormed the palace. By the time Queen Lili'uokalani accepted this condition, the U.S. Congress, influenced by the powerful people who wanted Lili'uokalani deposed, decided to move toward annexing Hawai'i to the United States. The reign of the Hawai'ian monarchy had come to an end.

By 1894 a provisional government was established in the islands with Sanford B. Dole as its president. Dole declared Hawai'i a republic. Although he did nothing about it, President Grover Cleveland was embarrassed by this turn of events. "As I look back upon the first steps in this miserable business, and as I contemplate the means used to complete the outrage, I am ashamed of the whole affair," he said.

In 1898 the U.S. Congress passed a resolution officially annexing
Hawai'i. Hawai'ians became full citizens of the United States in 1900, but
they had no official representation in the federal government in Washington.
Many Hawai'ians continued to resent the sugar growers, whose power had
only increased. "Sugar is King in Hawai'i to a far greater extent than cotton
was in the Old South," journalist Ray Stannard Balzer wrote after visiting the
islands in 1911. "Those rich, warm lands in all the islands are devoted
almost exclusively now to the production of sugar cane."

Some islanders began to work for statehood, but many people in the
United States resisted this action. Some argued against granting Hawai'i
statehood because they believed that the islands' Asian communities were
alien to the United States and its way of life. Resistance began to crumble
when Japanese airplanes attacked the naval base at Pearl Harbor on

December 7, 1941 causing devastating loss of life and destruction. With this surprise raid Hawai'ians became the only Americans to suffer an attack by a foreign power in the twentieth century. Americans saw Hawai'ians of all ethnic backgrounds pull together to help the United States to defeat Japan and to win the war.

Although they were intensely loyal to the United States, Japanese Americans in Hawai'i suffered a great deal of discrimination during World War II. There were too many of them on the islands to confine them in internment camps, as was done on the U.S. mainland. Instead, Japanese Americans living in Hawai'i had their activities restricted and watched. To be treated with such suspicion hurt the Japanese Americans on the islands. "Hawai'i is our home; the United States, our country. We know but one loyalty and that is to the Stars and Stripes. We wish to do our part as loyal Americans in every way possible, and we hereby offer ourselves for whatever service you may see fit to use us," stated 150 Hawai'ians of Japanese descent after they were dismissed from the Hawai'i Territorial Guard following the attack on Pearl Harbor.

Young Japanese Americans volunteered in great numbers to serve in the U.S. armed forces. One fighting unit, the 442nd Regimental Combat Team, was composed entirely of Japanese Americans and became the most decorated group of soldiers in the entire American army. "You fought not only the enemy but you fought prejudice—and you have won," President Harry S. Truman told the proud men of the 442nd as he honored them in Washington, D.C., after the war.

The long push for statehood eventually succeeded. Hawai'i became the fiftieth state in 1959. In the years since, this colorful society, with its many cultures and traditions, has become a model for how American citizens of different backgrounds can live together and prosper.

CONTEMPORARY HAWAI'I

In 1993, on the one hundredth anniversary of the overthrow of Queen Lili'uokalani, President Bill Clinton of the United States signed a formal apology to the people of Hawai'i in what is known as the United States Public Law 102-150, or the so-called Apology Resolution. With this statement, the U.S. government apologized for its role in the overthrow of Queen Lili'uokalani. The apology was based on James H. Blount's 1893 report for the then president Grover Cleveland, which had stated that the overthrow of the queen was illegal.

Some Native Hawai'ians are hoping that this formal statement will help in their bid to be recognized, as are Native Americans, as indigenous people with certain rights. Other Native Hawai'ians believe that the apology does not go far enough. They want more than just the status of indigenous rights. They want their sovereignty restored. They also believe that not just Native Hawai'ians (who are defined by bloodlines), but all national Hawai'ians (those who immigrated to the islands and are not of Polynesian blood) have been affected by the illegal overthrow and the taking away of their rights as an independent nation.

Senator Daniel Kahikina Akaka, a Native Hawai'ian, proposed a bill in 2000 called the Akaka Bill that would further guarantee indigenous rights to all Native Hawai'ians. The bill was approved by the U.S. Senate Indian Affairs Committee in 2005 and has now been presented to the full Senate for consideration. "This bill is important to everyone in Hawai'i," Senator Akaka said, "because it provides the structured process we need to begin to resolve the long-standing issues resulting from the overthrow of the Kingdom of Hawai'i."

The struggle for sovereignty continues in the Hawai'ian Islands. Groups such as ALOHA (Aboriginal Lands of Hawai'ian Ancestry), OHA (Office of

Hawai'ian Affairs), Ka Lahui, Ka Pakaukau, the Hawai'ian Kingdom, and the Nation of Hawai'i, all have members throughout the islands who are fighting for the government, lands, and control of their nation that was taken away from them. Each group has its own way of protesting against, or of appealing to, the U.S. government. Some of the groups camp out on public land in order to make their protest known. Some others work through waging legal battles. It was through the voices of some of these groups that pressure was applied upon the U.S. government, which ultimately led to the official apology of the United States signed by President Clinton.

The newest state of the Union has a history very much different from the rest of the country, making Hawai'i unique not only in its landscape and the ethnicity of its people, but also in how it became a state. Of all the states, Hawai'i is the only one in which its citizens are earnestly debating whether they want their homeland to remain a state. Like the volcanoes that created their island paradise, Hawai'i's concept of statehood is still forming.

The Aloha March is a demonstration by those who support annexation and an increase in sovereignty over the island.

Chapter Three

The People— Hawai'ian Style

Who are the real Hawai'ians? Hawai'ians have worked out their own answers to this difficult question. Hawai'ian businessman George Kanakele once explained it this way, "These days, any resident of this state who considers Hawai'i his home and who has an understanding of the values of Hawai'ian culture ought to consider himself or herself a Hawai'ian."

Hawai'ians live their lives and go about their daily work in much the same way as other American citizens. Nevertheless, this remote group of tropical islands, with its mix of Polynesian, Asian, and Western peoples, has its own unique culture and lifestyle.

MANY HAWAI'IANS

People from more than fifty different ethnic groups live in the Hawai'ian Islands. These include Japanese, Chinese, Koreans, Filipinos, Samoans,

More than 100,000 people claim to be Native Hawai'ian/Other Pacific Islander in Hawai'i.

Portuguese, Spaniards, Italians, Germans, Norwegians, Russians, English, Scots, Puerto Ricans, Mexicans, Guamanians, Vietnamese, Asian Indians, Native Americans, African Americans, and Native Hawai'ians. The strong Asian and Polynesian influences help to make Hawai'i's population unique among the states.

A large portion of the population has mixed ancestry, and their numbers are increasing, making Hawai'i the most racially integrated state in the nation. Many people believe that is why Hawai'i has fewer racial problems than other states. "Everybody's got a Japanese daughter-in-law or a Chinese son-in-law or a Filipino relative," said David A. Heenan, a white business-man whose wife is Filipino. "It's hard to throw stones at somebody when they're in the family." There is no majority ethnic group in Hawai'i—every group is a minority.

Of the almost two million people on the islands, an estimated 206,331 are of Japanese descent. The Japanese first arrived in 1868 when Japan was suffering economic problems. These early settlers called Hawai'i *Tenjiku*, the "heavenly place." By 1900, with a population of 60,000, they were the largest ethnic group in Hawai'i.

Today, the Japanese-American community is very successful in business and government. They celebrate their heritage several times during the year, beginning in March with Girls' Day. On that day it is customary to give young girls a doll, and the department stores are full of doll displays. During the eight-week Cherry Blossom Festival, there are demonstrations of Japanese arts, such as the tea ceremony, martial arts, flower arranging, and bonsai gardening. A cherry blossom queen is also crowned. When Boys' Day is celebrated on May 5, the sky is filled with colorful fish. Paper carps are flown from rooftops as symbols of strength and courage, and families fly a special carp kite for each son.

ETHNIC HAWAI'I

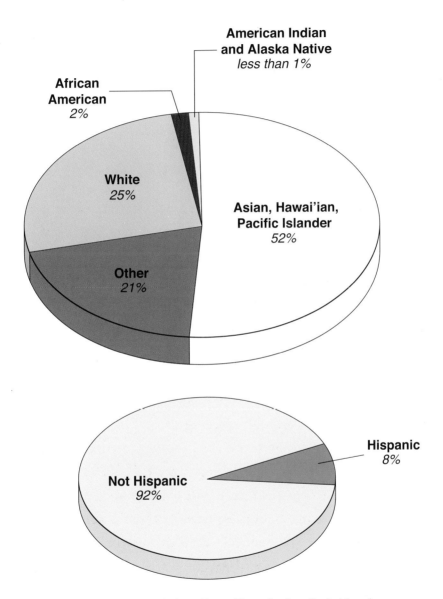

**American Indian
and Alaska Native**
less than 1%

**African
American**
2%

White
25%

**Asian, Hawai'ian,
Pacific Islander**
52%

Other
21%

Hispanic
8%

Not Hispanic
92%

*Note: A person of Cuban, Mexican, Puerto Rican, South or Central American,
or other Spanish culture or origin, regardless of race, is defined as Hispanic.*

Those of Japanese descent celebrate their heritage at the Pan-Pacific Parade Festival in Honolulu.

The Chinese had begun arriving in Hawai'i in great numbers in the 1850s when the sugar growers started importing labor from Asia. The Chinese called Hawai'i *Tan Hueng Shan*, or "land of the fragrant hills," after the pleasing aroma of the sandalwood trees that once grew in the islands.

It was estimated in 2004 that 51,144 Chinese Americans (with ancestors from mainland China, not Taiwan) now live in Hawai'i, mostly on the island of Oa'hu. In late January the Chinese New Year is celebrated. At that time the streets are filled with the sounds of exploding firecrackers, and huge paper lions snake their way through the streets, scaring away the bad spirits. The Chinese Hawai'ians also celebrate Buddha's birthday in April with formal tea ceremonies and traditional singing and dancing.

Almost 190,000 Hawai'ians are of Filipino ancestry. They came a little later than other groups, first arriving in 1906. Many Filipinos were brought in as strikebreakers when earlier Chinese and Japanese immigrants began to demand higher wages from the plantation owners. At first the established immigrants were prejudiced against them. Although the Filipinos soon organized and began to demand improved working conditions themselves along with their fellow Japanese immigrants, they remain among the poorest groups in the state today. In May they hold the Fiesta Filipina, which includes traditional foods, music and dance, exhibitions of handicrafts, and a beauty contest.

Hawai'i's small community of about 25,000 Korean Americans has integrated into the larger society more seamlessley than any other group. Their rate of intermarriage with other ethnic groups is high. Koreans first came to Hawai'i to work in the cane fields in the early 1900s.

Those who claim Native-Hawai'ian descent number about 68,000. All Hawai'ians celebrate King Kamehameha Day on June 11. It has become a state holiday, as has Prince Kuhio Day on March 26. The fall brings the colorful Aloha Festivals, which include parades, pageants, balls, and the coronation of a royal court at I'olani Palace. *Na Mele o Mau'i* is a one-day festival in December that is devoted to Hawai'ian culture. It features displays of native arts and crafts, canoe races, and luaus.

Performers dance at the Polynesian Cultural Center in O'ahu.

There are about 309,400 Caucasians (or 484,979, when mixed race Caucasians are included) in Hawai'i. Many are the descendants of European and American merchants, businesspeople, missionaries, sailors, and cane field workers. There are also many *malihini*, or new-comers—mostly white mainlanders who are drawn to the island state by its climate, scenery, and unique way of life.

Hawai'i's many groups have made widespread contributions to present-day Hawai'ian culture. This broad ethnic diversity is reflected in the language, varied foods, and colorful festivals that Hawai'ians enjoy.

SPEAKING HAWAI'IAN

The State of Hawai'i has two official languages: English and Hawai'ian. Although the Hawai'ian language is taught in some schools and universities, no more than two thousand residents of the islands still speak it fluently. Most of these people live on Ni'ihau, where the largest population of pure Hawai'ians still live. Other speakers include the elders of the islands' communities. Some children are enrolled in immersion schools where subjects are taught in Hawai'ian in an effort to keep the language alive. This program, however, has not been completely successful. One reason is that outside the schools the students have no one with whom to practice their new language skills.

While rarely spoken exclusively, many words of the Hawai'ian vocabulary are part of daily speech in the islands. Common words and place names are integrated into regular English speech. A committed effort is being made to keep proper use of both written and spoken Hawai'ian for present and future generations.

Historically, the Hawai'ian language was a spoken language only. The Hawai'ians had no alphabet, because they had no need to write anything down. In the early 1820s missionaries devised an alphabet for the Hawai'ian language as part of their efforts to Christianize the Hawai'ians. They translated, printed, and taught the Bible book by book. The New Testament was completed in 1832 and the Old Testament was finished in 1839.

The Hawai'ian language, which has the shortest alphabet in the world, has only twelve letters, the consonants *h, k, l, m, n, p,* and *w,* and the vowels *a, e, i, o,* and *u.* An apostrophe is included in the written form of some words, including place names, to indicate a brief, silent pause, called a glottal stop or, in Hawai'ian, an *'okina.* This is heard when a speaker pronounces *Hawai'i* the traditional way, saying, *h˘a - w¯ı - [glottal stop] - ¯e* . Actually, to say *Hawai'i* properly, you would pronounce the *w* as a *v,* as in: *h˘a - v¯ı - [glottal stop] - ¯e* .

Today, the English language is dominant in the state, with the state's native language contributing hundreds of words to everyday speech. Although English is spoken throughout all the islands, most often what is heard is really an English-Hawai'ian creole. A creole language is one that has developed from two or more languages. In Hawai'i this combination includes English, Hawai'ian, Portuguese, Japanese, Cantonese (a Chinese dialect), and Filipino words. The Hawai'ian pidgin, as it is called in the islands, came about from immigrant workers having to communicate with one another while being able to speak only their mother languages. The words and syntax, or grammar, from the different languages were mixed together to create what has become the English-Hawai'ian creole. Some typical phrases in Hawai'ian pidgin include: *that was ono,* which means, "that was very good tasting"; *all pau,* which means, "it's all done" or "it's all gone"; and *hele on,* which means "let's get moving" or "hurry up."

POPULATION DENSITY

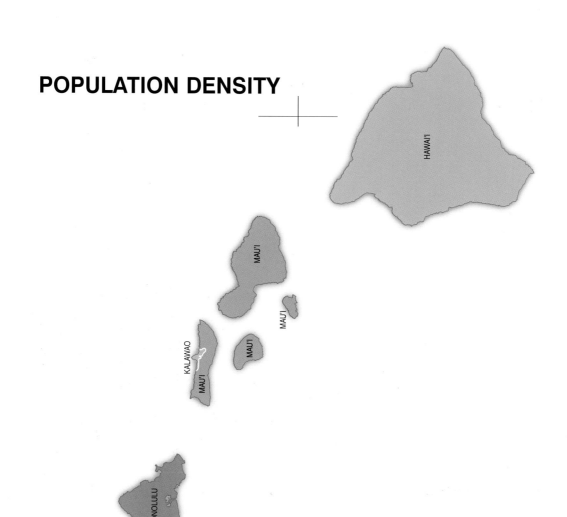

HAWAI'I

MAU'I

MAU'I

KALAWAO

MAU'I

MAU'I

HONOLULU

KAUA'I

KAUA'I

Persons per square mile

0.0 to 0.9
1 to 6.9
7 to 79.9
80 to 159.9
160 to 299.9
300 to 2,999.9
3,000 to 66,940

THE LEI

The first difference visitors might notice when they arrive in Hawai'i is the warm spirit of kindness and harmony that welcomes strangers into the community. This is the quality of aloha, or welcome, which is symbolized by the lei, a necklace woven of flowers that is given on special occasions and in welcome to many visitors upon arrival on any of the islands. There are many kinds of lei, made of a great variety of fresh flowers (from orchids to plumeria blossoms), berries, nuts, ferns, vines, leaves, shells, and even bird feathers. Before Western contact, the lei was used as an offering to the gods in sacred rituals and dances. Each island has its own style of lei making and its particular combination of materials. The most prized is the shell lei from Ni'ihau, which is more likely to be found in expensive jewelry shops and craft galleries than around the necks of visitors. The most common is a lei made of plumeria flowers, which are usually a light pink or white and have a very pleasant aroma.

THE LUAU

The most famous Hawai'ian gathering is the luau, a great feast staged to celebrate weddings, christenings, birthdays, and other important events.

Introduced by early Polynesian sailors, the lei was used as decoration and as a way to set themselves apart from others.

Nowadays, tourists can experience a commercialized version of the luau at almost any Hawai'ian hotel, but the traditional celebration involves family and friends and brings everyone together for several days to prepare the food and to enjoy the festive activities. Many traditional methods of cooking fish, meat, and vegetables are used at a luau. The meal can be eaten indoors or outdoors. It lasts for the entire evening, as a huge display of food is laid out before the guests on a bed of banana leaves or bamboo mats.

The main dish at a luau is usually pork. A pig is wrapped in ti leaves and roasted in an *imu*, an earthen pit filled with kiawe wood and hot lava stones. When the pig is finished being cooked, it is placed on a table and usually surrounded by foods such as taro, breadfruit, and yams. The rest of the food might include the many fruits native to the islands—papayas, mangoes, guavas, passion fruit, litchis, kumquats, tamarinds, and pineapples.

A luau offers a variety of foods laid out for all to enjoy.

MACADAMIA NUT COOKIES

Hawai'i is renowned for its macadamia nuts, which can be found in U.S. supermarkets. Adding them to recipes is an easy way to make regular food a little bit more special. An adult should help with this recipe.

2 cups flour
1 cup soft butter
1/2 cup brown sugar
2 eggs
1 teaspoon grated orange peel
1 cup chopped macadamia nuts

Mix the flour, butter, sugar, eggs, and orange peel until the batter is smooth. Stir in the nuts. Chill the dough for half an hour. Put the dough between two pieces of wax paper and roll it out until it is about 1/4 inch thick. Cut the dough into 2-inch squares and place 1 1/2 inches apart on a lightly greased cookie sheet. Bake at 325 degrees for about 20 minutes. The cookies are ready when they're golden.

Fish dishes may include *onaga* (snapper), ahi (yellowfin tuna), or mahimahi (dolphin fish, not the mammal dolphin). There also might be octopus, prawns, or lobsters.

The taro root produces another popular Hawai'ian dish certain to be served at luaus. This is poi. The taro is baked, mashed to a pulp, strained, and eaten as a gray paste. It is a starchy food that takes the place of potatoes or bread in a mainland diet. It is often eaten out of a calabash shell. The feast usually concludes with a dessert of haupia, a coconut pudding.

MUSIC AND DANCE

With its catchy melodies and poetic lyrics, Hawai'ian music is immensely popular. The most famous musical instrument, the ukulele, evolved from the *machete,* a type of guitar taken to the islands by Portuguese who immigrated to work in the cane fields. In Hawai'ian, *ukulele* means "jumping flea," a colorful description of how the instrument sounds.

Other unique musical instruments that are typically used to accompany traditional hula are the *kalaau,* two wooden sticks that produce the tone of a xylophone; the *ili ili,* stone clappers; the *pu ili,* split bamboo sticks; and the *ipu,* a pair of hollow gourds. The steel guitar is an essential part of any modern Hawai'ian ensemble. It was invented by Joseph Kekuku in the 1880s. What gives much of Hawai'ian music its unique sound, however, is the slack-key style of playing, in which the strings of the guitar are tuned to notes slightly lower than standard guitar tuning.

The dance most closely associated with Hawai'ian music is the hula. It is a traditional Hawai'ian dance, performed in ancient times in worship of Laka, the sister of the fire goddess, Pele. Early in Polynesian and Hawai'ian history the hula was danced only by men in religious ceremonies. It required a great deal of training and practice to master the more than two hundred

Women entertain visitors with the sounds of their ukuleles.

dances and their accompanying chants, all used to convey narrative accounts of gods and wars, legends and love stories.

As men became more preoccupied with making war, women took over the hula traditions. The first missionaries disapproved of the hula because they thought it was too sexually provocative, and for a time they succeeded in preventing its performance. The dance was revived by King David Kalakaua. Today, hula thrives as popular commercial entertainment as well as a serious art form performed in the traditional manner by Hawai'ian dancers who are interested in preserving their culture. Hula schools and *kumu hula*, or hula masters, present their dances during festivals. On a competitive level, the most serious dancers and teachers gather in Hilo once a year to showcase their skills at the Merrie Monarch Festival.

In the nineteenth century Hawai'ian royalty had a profound impact on the islanders' music. In 1836 King Kamehameha III established the Royal Hawai'ian Band and in 1872 the conductor's baton was passed to Heinrich (Henry) Berger. The German bandmaster became known as the father of Hawai'ian music. In his forty-odd years as bandleader, he arranged more than one thousand Hawai'ian songs for performance, composed seventy-five original songs, and conducted more than 30,000 concerts. The Royal Hawai'ian Band still performs public concerts every week on the grounds of the I'olani Palace.

From the 1930s to the 1960s Hawai'ian music, or a Western imitation of it, was popular throughout the world. Over the years more modern versions of Hawai'ian music have absorbed influences from jazz, ragtime, blues, and Latin music. Today, rock and roll has captured the imagination of many Hawai'ian performers. But there are also young musicians, part of a growing movement of culturally conscious people, who continue to compose and to perform in traditional styles.

Native Hawai'ians believe that the hula was first performed by a god or goddess, making the dance a sacred ritual.

HAWAI'IAN CLOTHING

In the earliest times, before woven cloth was introduced in the islands, Hawai'ians wore clothes that were made from plant materials. Typically, men wore loincloths wrapped around the lower part of their torsos. The material used was often tapa cloth, which was made from the inner bark of wauke (paper mulberry) trees. Tapa cloth is a Polynesian invention, found in Samoa, Tonga, Fiji, and New Zealand, as well as in Hawai'i.

Missionaries who came to the islands after 1820 found the clothing that Hawai'ian women were wearing (usually just a skirt with no top) too suggestive. The missionary women got together and created the mu'umu'u(below), a long, loose-fitting dress that hides the female figure under yards of brightly colored material. Mu'umu'us are still worn in Hawai'i but mostly by older women on traditional occasions.

Later, around the turn of the twentieth century, the *palaka* was the clothing style that was most often seen not only in the sugarcane fields, but along the streets of the developing villages and towns in Hawai'i.

The palaka, Hawai'ian for plaid, usually made in a blue and white pattern, used the durable material of denim (like blue jeans material) so it would withstand the rugged wear of laborers. This along with denim trousers called sailor-mokus became standard wear, so popular that some people referred to it as the national costume of the islands.

Later still, Japanese fashion styles influenced clothing as the twentieth century moved on. Patterns taken from the Japanese kimono were painted onto silk, and this material was used to fashion shirts and dresses for Hawai'ians. In the late 1930s the artist Elsie Das was commissioned to create a uniquely Hawai'ian design for fabrics. She painted several floral prints, which were sent to Japan, where they were printed by hand onto silk. This material was then sent back to the islands and made into what would eventually inspire the aloha shirt (above), the popular shirts that are seen all over the islands today. Pictures of hibiscus, ginger, plumeria, orchids, birds of paradise flowers, and pineapples are popular images found on aloha shirts as well as dresses, bathing suits, and shorts.

Today, clothing fashion leans toward the leisure side in Hawai'i. Casual Fridays that are popular on the U.S. mainland probably were inspired by the casual attitude of Hawai'ian businesspeople. In Hawai'i, Fridays are often referred to as Aloha Friday, when everyone is encouraged to wear the Hawai'ian trademark—the colorful aloha shirt.

To Hawai'ians, surfing was known as he'enalu. "He" means to slide; nalu means wave.

RIDING THE WAVES

Although Hawai'ians enjoy many different sports, there is one that originated in the islands—the ancient sport of *he'enalu*, or surfing. Surfing is mentioned in Hawai'ian songs dating back to the fifteenth century. When Captain Cook arrived in 1778, his men marveled at how the Hawai'ians seemed to glide so effortlessly on the powerful, rolling waves.

In those days the Hawai'ian nobility used 16-foot boards weighing as much as 150 pounds. Many of the best surfing beaches were reserved exclusively for the nobles' use. The commoners used shorter boards, which were about 6 feet long. The missionaries discouraged surfing, and interest in the sport waned as the native population declined and their way of life became more Westernized. Then in the early twentieth century Hawai'ians revived the sport. Today's surfboards are smaller and lighter and are often made of synthetic materials. The sport is known worldwide, with international competitions held in places like Hawai'i; Virginia Beach, Virginia; and Newcastle, Australia.

UA MAU KE EA O KA AINA I KA PONO

Chapter Four

Governing Hawai'i

Hawai'i became the fiftieth state on August 21, 1959, by a proclamation signed by President Dwight D. Eisenhower. In his speech honoring this occasion, President Eisenhower said, "We know that she [Hawai'i] is ready to do her part to make this Union a stronger nation—a stronger people than it was before because of her presence as a full sister to the other forty-nine states. So all of us say to her, 'good luck.' "

There were sixty-six years and countless heated debates about Hawai'i's statehood between the U.S. overthrow of Queen Liliuokalani to Hawai'i's becoming a state. Moreover, the controversy of statehood remains a seriously discussed issue in the islands today. At this time, however, Hawai'i's current government is modeled after those of the other forty-nine states, with a state constitution, federal representation in Washington, D.C., and a state government, which is centered in the state's capitol, Honolulu. Like all states, Hawai'i's government is divided into three branches: executive, legislative, and judicial.

The Hawai'ian state seal hangs in front of the I'olani Palace. It is patterned after the royal coat of arms of the kingdom of Hawai'i.

EXECUTIVE

The executive branch is headed by the governor, who is elected for a four-year term. The governor can recommend legislation and veto (reject) bills passed by the legislature. The governor also appoints top officials such as attorney general, finance director, and judges.

Some recent governors include John Waihee, who served from 1986 to 1994 and was the first governor of Hawai'ian ancestry. During his tenure Hawai'i became the first state in the Union to adopt universal health care. He was known also for promoting cooperation between government and private landowners in striving to protect Hawai'i's delicate environment.

Benjamin J. Cayetano, who served as governor from 1994 to 2002, was the first Filipino-American governor of any state. He was born in Honolulu into a poor immigrant family. "I don't remember hardship," Cayetano once said, "but if you've never tasted steak, you never know what you're missing." Cayetano went to college, became a lawyer, and entered politics. As governor, he worked hard to promote Hawai'i's interests during a difficult economic period. He once said, "When you're an elected official, you're given a great privilege and a great burden. You need to feel a sense of urgency about what you do."

Governor Linda Lingle works to "expand and diversify the economy and return fiscal discipline to government."

In 2002 Hawai'i scored another first by electing Linda Lingle as the first woman governor of the state. Some of the programs that Governor Lingle has proposed are aiding Hawai'i's homeless people, improving teacher shortages in the islands, and lessening the state's reliance on oil by developing renewable sources of energy.

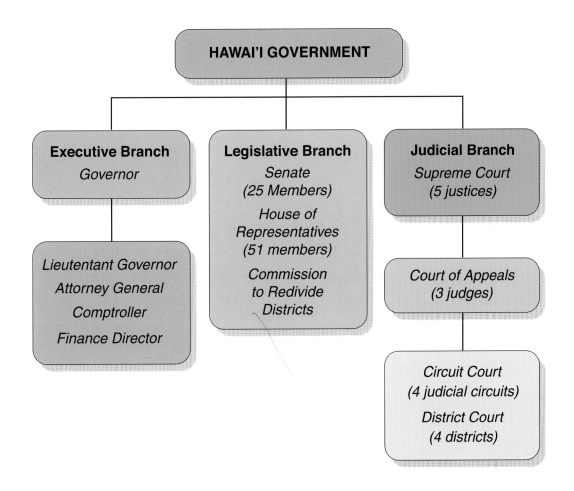

HAWAI'I GOVERNMENT

Executive Branch
Governor

Lieutentant Governor
Attorney General
Comptroller
Finance Director

Legislative Branch
Senate
(25 Members)

House of
Representatives
(51 members)

Commission
to Redivide
Districts

Judicial Branch
Supreme Court
(5 justices)

Court of Appeals
(3 judges)

Circuit Court
(4 judicial circuits)

District Court
(4 districts)

LEGISLATIVE

The Hawai'ian legislature is composed of a senate, with twenty-five members elected for four-year terms, and a house of representatives, with fifty-one members elected for two-year terms. A majority vote in both the house and senate is required to pass a bill, which is then sent to the governor for approval or veto. The legislature can overturn a veto if two-thirds of the members agree. The senate also approves the appointments made by the governor.

JUDICIAL

The role of the Hawai'ian court system is to administer justice impartially. Hawai'i has many district and circuit courts and a family court. If disputants disagree with a decision made by any of these courts, they may ask the intermediate court of appeals to overturn the ruling. Further appeals can be taken to the state supreme court, the highest court in Hawai'i.

LOCAL GOVERNMENT

Hawai'i is unusual in that it has no city governments. The city of Honolulu is the state capital, but it is governed as part of Honolulu County, which includes the entire island of O'ahu. Each county has a mayor and council. These county governments provide vital services such as police and firefighters, which cities provide in other states.

A statue of King Kamehameha I stands in front of Hawai'i's state judiciary building in Honolulu.

HAWAI'I BY COUNTY

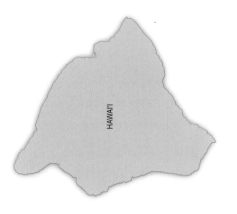

HAWAI'I

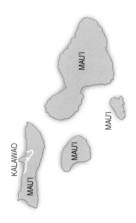

MAUI

MAUI

KALAWAO

MAUI

MAUI

HONOLULU

KAUA'I

KAUA'I

THE NATIVE SOVEREIGNTY MOVEMENT

Some Native Hawai'ians still question whether the islands should be part of the United States. They believe they should govern themselves. The Native-Hawai'ian sovereignty movement is the central issue in Hawai'ian politics today.

Though only about 9,000 Hawai'ians can claim pure Hawai'ian ancestry, there are over 200,000 people who are partly Native Hawai'ian. They call themselves the *kanaka maoli*. As a group, they have the lowest income, the shortest life expectancy, the highest rate of infant mortality, and the lowest level of education.

Lilikala Kame'eleihiwa, a Hawai'ian author, summed up the attitude of many kanaka maoli when she said, "We are an occupied people." Although some people liken the plight of the Native Hawai'ians to that of Native Americans elsewhere in the United States, many Native Hawai'ians resent such comparisons. They point out that their heritage and history are unique. "First they made us Hawai'ians, then they said we're Americans; now they want to make us Indian?" demanded Michael Grace, a kanaka maoli activist.

Many different groups have taken up the cause of Hawai'ian sovereignty. In early 1994 a coalition of these groups met at the I'olani Palace, the royal palace of the Hawai'ian monarchy, and issued the Proclamation of Restoration of the Independence of the Sovereign Nation-State of Hawai'i. By early 1995 they had agreed on a constitution for their new nation. Though these documents do not have the force of law, they have caused a great deal of political controversy.

Native Hawai'ian groups disagree about what kind of independence they should have. Some think they should have a nation within a nation, similar to a Native American Indian reservation. Others are

Construction of the I'olani Palace was completed in 1882. It was the official residence of Hawai'i's royalty.

demanding reparations and the return of the lands held in trust for them by the state and federal governments. Much of that land has been developed as state parks, private farms and ranches, and beachfront resorts, thus many complications would arise. Still other kanaka maoli groups are demanding complete independence, restoration of the Hawai'ian monarchy, restrictions on the immigration of non-Hawai'ians, and the denial of voting rights to non-Hawai'ian residents.

Chapter Five

Working in the Islands

Hawai'ians, like people everywhere, are concerned about whether their economy will remain strong enough to provide well-paid jobs for the state's citizens and a bright future for its children. For several recent decades Hawai'i has been one of the nation's most prosperous states. The average per capita income in Hawai'i is $34,539, the same as the national average (in 2005, Hawai'i ranked nineteenth in all the states for per capita personal income), and the unemployment rate is consistently lower than the national average (lowest of all states in 2006). In terms of the cost of living, however, Hawai'i is one of the most expensive places to live, due largely to the high cost of housing and food.

THE HIGH PRICE OF PARADISE

Some of the factors that make Hawai'i special also give it special problems. As an island state almost 3,000 miles off the American mainland, Hawai'i must import a great many items from automobiles to building materials to food, clothing, and medicine. This accounts for a higher-than-usual cost of living in the state.

Agriculture is one of the smallest industry sectors in Hawai'i accounting for less than 1 percent of the state's income and 2 percent of employment.

Ships unload their cargo at the Port of Honolulu.

The state's natural beauty also indirectly contributes to the high cost of living. Hawai'ians are very concerned with preserving their spectacular landscape, and a huge percentage of the state's land is owned or maintained by the government. That makes the small amount of available land very expensive. Furthermore, in the 1980s there was a huge amount of resort and hotel development. As investors bought up the land, housing prices skyrocketed, doubling between 1986 and 1990. Hawai'i now has some of the highest-priced real estate in the world.

2004 GROSS STATE PRODUCT: $50 Million

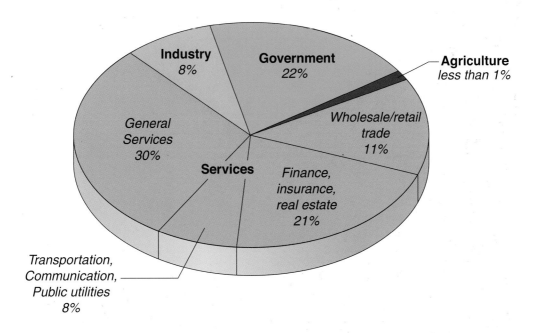

HAWAI'I'S CHALLENGES

Hawai'i is growing more urban, and big-city problems such as crime and homelessness seem unavoidable. A visitor to Hawai'i might be surprised to learn that although the crime rate has been on the decline over the past decade, it still remains high in comparison with other American states. Most of Hawai'i's crimes are nonviolent offenses such as burglary and theft. The rate of violent crime is among the lowest in the country.

Another urban problem that plagues Hawai'ians living in the more populated areas is the congestion from heavy traffic. Many people who live in Honolulu's outskirts have grown used to eating their breakfast while crawling along at 15 miles per hour during their 90-minute morning commute.

Honolulu is focused on solving the problem of how to move people rather than how to move cars. Improved public transit is being planned.

Honolulu is located on a flat coastal plain where most of its commercial and industrial industries have been developed.

Honolulu also consistently ranks as one of the best U.S. cities for walking and bicycling. The number of cars keeps rising, however, and most of O'ahu between the mountains and the beach has been developed, so there is nowhere to build new highways. "We're pretty much resigned to the fact that state engineers are never going to solve the traffic problems," said David Nagata. "This is a very small island for the amount of people who live here, and there are no limits on the amount of cars. Traffic is a way of life on O'ahu." But he has no intention of moving. "I like the life here," he said. Traffic has become a problem on Mau'i, too.

HAWAI'I WORKFORCE

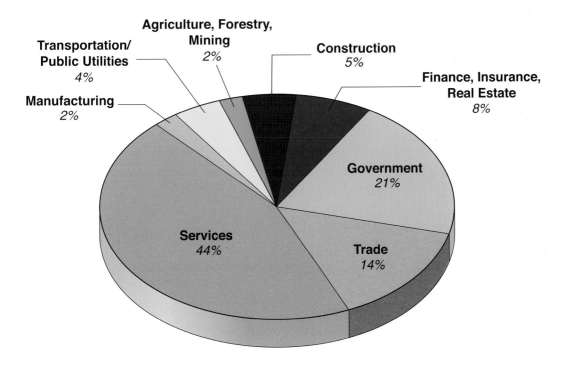

Transportation/ Public Utilities 4%

Agriculture, Forestry, Mining 2%

Construction 5%

Finance, Insurance, Real Estate 8%

Manufacturing 2%

Government 21%

Services 44%

Trade 14%

HAWAI'I TODAY AND TOMORROW

New business opportunities and an inviting climate have caused the population of Hawai'i to grow quickly during the last decade. Tourism changed the face of Hawai'i as millions of jet-age travelers began to discover for themselves the islands' magnificent beaches and scenery. Tourism is now the state's largest industry. In the month of January 2006 alone, more than half a million people visited the islands and spent $1 billion while they were there.

Tourism ranks as Hawai'i's biggest industry. Many visitors flock to the famous Waikiki Beach for sun, surf, and sand.

Soldiers train on a Hawai'ian beach.

The second-largest sector of the economy is the U.S. military, which contributes about $5 billion to the state annually. The military deploys all the services there, with more than 40,000 uniformed men and women stationed in Hawai'i, about 15,000 civilian support workers, and some 60,000 dependents of military personnel. In no other state do armed-forces personnel and their families make up such a large percentage of the population. Changes in the nation's military policy often directly affect Hawai'ians, because any reduction in military spending can hurt the Hawai'ian economy.

Though agriculture no longer dominates, it is still the third-largest contributor to the Hawai'ian economy. The state's major exports are sugar, pineapples, cattle, coffee, papayas, bananas, and cut flowers. Hawai'i is also the world's second-largest producer of macadamia nuts (Australia is first). The once mighty sugar industry, although still important, has been humbled. After decades of labor struggles, the men and women who work in the cane fields have become highly paid workers. As a result, sugarcane production has been slowly shifting to low-wage countries such as the Philippines and Taiwan.

Located on the Big Island 3,000 feet above sea level, the Kahua Ranch raises cattle, sheep, and horses.

EARNING A LIVING

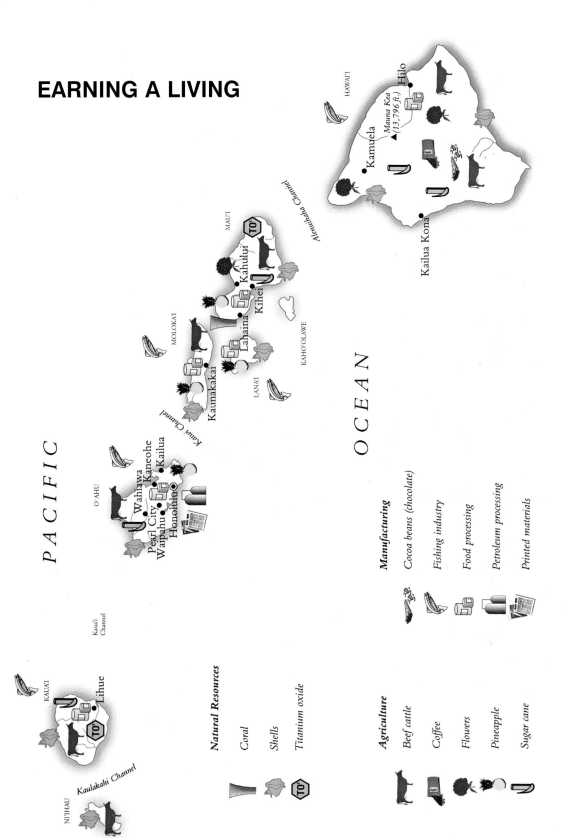

HAWAI'I

Hilo
Mauna Kea
(13,796 ft.)
Kamuela
Kailua Kona

MAUI

TO'
Kahului
Kihei
Lahaina

MOLOKA'I

Kaunakakai

LANAI

KAHO'OLAWE

Alenuihaha Channel

O'AHU

Wahiawa
Kaneohe
Kailua
Pearl City
Waipahu
Honolulu

Kaua'i Channel

Kau'i Channel

KAUA'I

Lihue

TO'

NI'IHAU

Kaulakahi Channel

PACIFIC

OCEAN

Natural Resources

Coral

Shells

TO' Titanium oxide

Manufacturing

Cocoa beans (chocolate)

Fishing industry

Food processing

Petroleum processing

Printed materials

Agriculture

Beef cattle

Coffee

Flowers

Pineapple

Sugar cane

During the 1970s and 1980s Japanese investors purchased a great deal of real estate in Hawai'i. Although that created an economic boom, some Hawai'ians were ambivalent about it. "The immediate effect of Japanese hotel development on Mau'i was the increased urbanization of our shorelines and loss of open beaches," said Mau'i resident Dana Noane Hall. She believed that many Hawai'ians "feel trapped by having to support an industry that may give them a job, but that takes away from their ability to enjoy the place they live—to dive, to fish, to swim. Instead, they get to look at a glossy brochure of out-of-state residents doing what they used to do."

A recession in the early 1990s in Japan reduced Japanese investment and hurt the Hawai'ian economy. Japanese tourism was also affected by the recession, and Hawai'i felt the pinch. The terrorist attacks on the U.S. mainland in 2001 also affected tourism, as many people were afraid to fly. In addition, the high price of oil, which is eventually reflected in higher air fares, dampened the tourism trade.

In 2004 and 2005, however, the economy turned around as Hawai'i enjoyed the benefits of record-breaking numbers of people visiting the islands. No one knows for sure if this will last, though, so alternative methods of bolstering the economy are being sought.

One such venture is opening up Pearl Harbor as a commercial dry dock, where cruise line companies could dock their ships for maintenance. The construction industry is also booming in Hawai'i, as more people and more businesses move to the islands and need new homes and office buildings. Hawai'i, through its universities and its business sector, is also working hard to train workers in advanced technologies in order to develop strong and productive environments for science research and other projects in the state. Hawai'i hopes to become an international leader in such fields as information technology, telecommunications, medical technology, and astronomy, to name just a few. Of special interest is the field of renewable energy sources.

Hawai'i is the most oil-dependent state in the Union. With prices rising rapidly and oil supplies becoming scarce, Hawai'i's government has struck a bold new stance in the state's need for energy. In changing from oil-based energy to solar, wind, or other renewable sources, Hawai'i hopes to lead the nation in building more reliance on low-cost, sustainable energy. Changing from oil-based energy could not only save the state billions of dollars, it could also help to protect the environment, as fuels other than oil can be used without dumping millions of tons of carbon dioxide into the air. The state's plan to invest in alternative fuels has met with approval from the federal government, which has provided funds so that researchers in Hawai'i can go forward with their studies. Hawai'i has many natural possibilities for energy other than solar and wind. Geothermal energy from the heat of hot lava, as well as energy produced by wave action are but two forms that are under study. Other research is being done on totally electric vehicles that produce zero (or near zero) emissions and on working with hydrogen-based fuels.

With these innovations Hawai'i might not only lead the nation in the use of cleaner and lower-cost fuels, but may also boost its economy both by saving money and by being the first to discover better and more efficient energy technologies. The sun and the colorful landscape are not the only bright things in the Hawai'ian Islands. The future is also shining.

In South Point, on the island of Hawai'i, Kamoa Wind Farm generates electricity with the power of its huge windmills.

Chapter Six

A Tour of the Islands

Over seven million visitors traveled to the Hawai'ian Islands in 2005, and their numbers are climbing. The tourists come in search of warm, sunny beaches, dramatic tropical scenery, and a relaxed pace of life. Hawai'i is a paradise for lovers of the outdoors. The islands offer magnificent opportunities for swimming, surfing, deep-sea and blue water fishing, hiking, camping, scuba diving, rock climbing, horseback riding, sailing, bicycle riding, golf, and tennis.

HONOLULU

Most visitors to Hawai'i today arrive by ocean liners or airplanes. There are about 80,000 tourists on O'ahu on any given day, and their first experience of the islands is likely to be the capital city of Honolulu.

Downtown Honolulu is the site of historic symbols of ancient Hawai'ian culture, including the I'olani Palace, where the last Hawai'ian monarchs ruled before their kingdom was overthrown. Behind the palace and dwarfing it is the state capitol, which was built in 1969. At the state judicial building, Ali'iolani Hale, stands a statue of King Kamehameha I. On June 11, Kamehameha Day, the statue is adorned with a long flower lei.

Kayak tours are a great way to explore the islands.

June 11 is the day honoring King Kamehameha I.

Another interesting Honolulu site is Washington Place, a former home of Queen Lili'uokalani that was the residence of Hawai'i's governors until 2002, when a new governor's home was built. Washington Place is still used for official functions and is being restored as a museum. Kawaiahao Church was completed by the Christian missionary Hiram Bingham in 1842 and was constructed from large blocks of coral cut out from nearby reefs. Along the city's southern shore is the famous natural feature Diamond Head, the monumental remnant of an extinct crater 760 feet above the ocean.

Honolulu also has many fascinating museums. The Bishop Museum features frequently changing exhibitions depicting Polynesian culture. The museum also has a science center with a planetarium and observatory. The Honolulu Academy of Arts has an excellent collection of Asian art, as well as a fine collection of works by Western Impressionist painters.

Waikiki Beach is a 2.5-mile strip of sandy beaches, reefs, and coconut groves that has become a world-famous resort area. It has been an important destination for tourists since the 1920s. Since the 1950s, a line of large hotels, known as the Great Wall of Waikiki, has encircled the beach. There are more than 30,000 hotel rooms in the Waikiki area. Near the beach is the International Market Place, an acre of land devoted to restaurants and cafés, small shops, and kiosks selling tourist items. The more than eight hundred restaurants, bars, and clubs near Waikiki make it a place for people who prefer urban nightlife after a day of seeing Hawai'i's tropical scenery, though the glowing orange sunsets along Waikiki beach are magnificent.

Kapiolani Park is probably Honolulu's most popular park. Close below Diamond Head, it features tennis courts and soccer fields as well as fields for other sports. The historic Royal Hawai'ian Band plays there on Sunday afternoons. There is a large zoo, an aviary, an aquarium, a rose garden, picnic tables, and a beach.

Honolulu offers many interesting neighborhoods to explore, particularly Chinatown, where there are Buddhist temples, Taoist shrines, herb and noodle shops, and busy open-air markets. Another fascinating site is the Punchbowl, a volcanic crater where human sacrifices were once conducted by the ancient Hawai'ians and is now the site of a national cemetery. North of the Punchbowl is Nu'uanu Pali Lookout, a cliff that offers outstanding views of the valleys north of the city.

The Punchbowl is a crater that contains the National Memorial Cemetery of the Pacific where graves of World War II, Korean, and Vietnam soldiers lay to rest.

TEN LARGEST CITIES

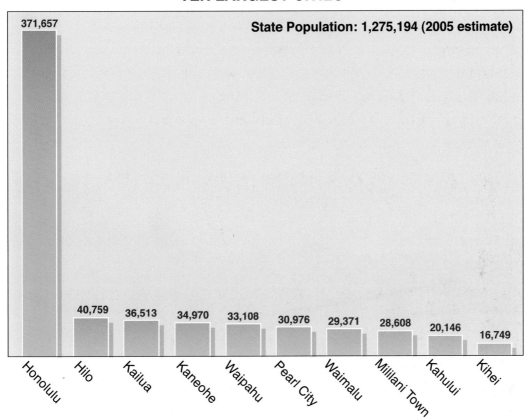

State Population: 1,275,194 (2005 estimate)

371,657 — Honolulu
40,759 — Hilo
36,513 — Kailua
34,970 — Kaneohe
33,108 — Waipahu
30,976 — Pearl City
29,371 — Waimalu
28,608 — Mililani Town
20,146 — Kahului
16,749 — Kihei

THE BIG ISLAND

Hawai'i, the Big Island, is the place to visit if you're interested in volcanoes. Its famous black sand beaches are made of lava that was slowly ground up by the sea. One of the island's two main volcanoes, Mauna Kea, has been extinct for thousands of years. On its slopes are many ancient Polynesian temples and the Mauna Kea adze quarry, where the first Hawai'ians mined a very hard basalt to make tools. Today, skiers take advantage of its snow-covered slopes. At the summit of Mauna Kea, scientists from the United States,

Canada, England, Japan, France, Argentina, Australia, Brazil, the Netherlands, and Taiwan have constructed thirteen huge astronomical telescopes. They include the largest optical/infrared telescopes in the world, the Keck telescopes, and the largest submillimeter telescope in the world, the James Clerk Maxwell Telescope.

Punalu'u Beach on the Big Island is one of Hawai'i's most beautiful black sand beaches.

The other major volcano on the island of Hawai'i, Mauna Loa, is not dormant—it is very much alive and has erupted thirty-three times in the last two centuries. Its last major eruption was in 1984, when lava flows stopped just 4 miles short of Hilo, the island's largest city. The west coast of Hawai'i features large expanses of solidified lava from Mauna Loa's eruptions in 1907, 1919, 1926, and 1950.

East of Mauna Loa is the crater of Kilauea volcano. Although Kilauea is not nearly as big as Mauna Kea and Mauna Loa, it is the most active volcano in the world. Fiery red lava has been pouring from its side since 1983. "Imagine the Mississippi [River] converted into liquid fire," said a witness at the 1840 eruption. At the southern edge of the caldera of Kilauea is Halemaumau, the volcano's main vent, about 280 feet deep and bubbling with flaming rock.

The city of Hilo, on the northeast coast, is the state's second-largest city, but it has not been built up with tourist hotels to the same extent as Honolulu. With its narrow streets and wooden houses, it has the appearance of a small, old-fashioned town. Tsunamis, or tidal waves, destroyed many of Hilo's buildings in 1946 and 1960, but much of the old historic district has been restored. Hilo is the center of the Hawai'ian orchid industry. More than two thousand varieties of the flower adorn the city's many gardens and parks. Especially worth visiting are the Lili'uokalani Gardens. For early risers, it is also exciting to watch the morning auction at the Suisan Fish Market.

Driving north out of Hilo along the Hamakua coast toward the magnificent Waipio Valley, many old sugar plantations and the towns that sprang up to serve the cane workers can still be seen. Macadamia nuts are grown on many of these plantations now.

PLACES TO SEE

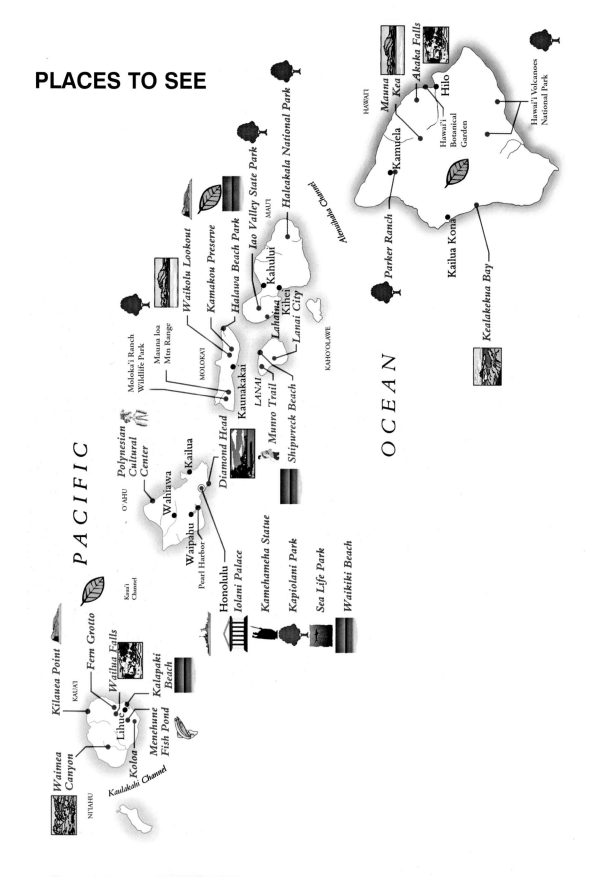

Waimea Canyon
Kilauea Point
Fern Grotto
Wailua Falls
Kalapaki Beach
Lihue
Menehune Fish Pond
Koloa
NIIHAU
KAUAI
Kauai Channel
Kaulakahi Channel

PACIFIC

Polynesian Cultural Center
Wahiawa
Kailua
Waipahu
Pearl Harbor
Honolulu
Iolani Palace
Kamehameha Statue
Kapiolani Park
Sea Life Park
Waikiki Beach
Diamond Head
O'AHU

Molokai Ranch Wildlife Park
Mauna Ioa Mtn Range
Waikolu Lookout
Kamakou Preserve
Halawa Beach Park
Kaunakakai
MOLOKAI
Munro Trail
Shipwreck Beach
LANAI
Lanai City
Lahaina
Kahului
Kihei
Iao Valley State Park
Haleakala National Park
KAHO'OLAWE
MAUI
Alenuihaha Channel

OCEAN

Mauna Kea
Akaka Falls
Hilo
Kamuela
Hawai'i Botanical Garden
Hawai'i Volcanoes National Park
Parker Ranch
Kailua Kona
Kealakekua Bay
HAWAI'I

MAU'I, MOLOKA'I, AND KAUA'I

Mau'i is the site of more astonishing volcanoes. Pu'u Kukui is almost 6,000 feet high, and Haleakala towers to just over 10,000 feet. The central crater of Haleakala is nearly 3,000 feet deep and has a circumference of about 15 miles. It is part of Haleakala National Park, which has many trails that can be traveled on foot or horseback. To watch the sun rise from the summit of Haleakala is an awe-inspiring sight. At Haleakala's summit is Science City, a group of laboratories where scientists track satellites and the University of Hawai'i operates solar observatories.

A hiker takes in the volcanic landscape in Haleakala National Park on the Cinder Cone Trail.

Lahaina, on Mau'i's western coast, has been popular with visitors since the early nineteenth century, when it was a favorite port of call for the American whaling fleet. The town retains some of the atmosphere of that time, with a mixture of old houses and modern cafés, restaurants, boutiques, and art galleries. Whales are often still seen to the south of Lahaina in Ma'alaea Bay.

Moloka'i is a small island west of Mau'i that is about 40 miles long and 7 miles wide. There are relatively few paved roads, and the population is less than seven thousand. The people of Moloka'i are committed to preventing the kind of overdevelopment some of the other islands have suffered. Instead of building resorts, some islanders want to develop hiking trails and camping areas. "By keeping Moloka'i unique, we will have a really good shot at attracting people in the future," said DeGray Vanderbilt, of the Moloka'i Chamber of Commerce. "But if we were to homogenize like the rest of the islands and roll over to indiscriminate development, we would be the big loser."

The most notable landmark of Moloka'i is at the Kalaupapa site of what was once a leper colony, where Father Joseph de Veuster, a Belgian Catholic priest known as Father Damien, the "Martyr of Moloka'i," worked with the lepers, starting in 1873. He himself died of leprosy, now referred to as Hansen's disease, in 1889.

Farther east, near the town of Halawa, some of the highest sea cliffs in the world tower over the waves that crash at their feet, with several waterfalls cascading more than 1,000 feet down from the mountains.

The island of Kaua'i is a hiker's and naturalist's paradise. The high peaks at its center, Waialeale and Kawaikini, can be bathed in nearly 500 inches of rainfall a year, making this the wettest spot on the planet.

Moloka'i's sea cliffs form the dramatic coast of the island's north shore.

The Kalalau Trail in Nā Pali Coast State Park is an 11-mile hike through lush valleys and along towering sea cliffs.

The rains cascade down the western slopes of these peaks into the Alakai Swamp, a splendid area of tropical rain forest and bogs where many of Hawai'i's rare trees and birds reside. Below the Alakai Swamp is Kokee State Park, which has wonderful views of the surrounding lowlands. The flow of water culminates in the Waimea Canyon. In Lihue, the main town on the island, the Kaua'i Museum holds demonstrations of weaving and lei making.

LAST IMPRESSIONS

To visit Hawai'i, then, is to confirm the fabulous images that millions of people cherish of these beautiful islands. This newest state evokes thoughts of a slightly mysterious paradise, a land of rugged volcanic mountains, dense tropical rain forests, coconut groves, flower lei, and sunny beaches with pounding surf.

But Hawai'i is more than the beautiful landscape. Hawai'i is a true melting pot. Halfway between North America and Asia, the state of Hawai'i—in geography, in history, and in its people and their cultures—stands as a bridge between East and West. By taking the best of each of the diversified cultures that have come together to create Hawai'i, the people of this state might indeed lead the way through the twenty-first century to a new way of dealing with nature, the environment, and everyday life. They might do this by using the lessons they have learned from the islands' sometimes turbulent history and by teaching others what it truly means to share the Hawai'ian Aloha Spirit.

THE FLAG: The state flag of Hawai'i contains both the British flag and the American flag. In the upper left-hand corner of the Hawai'ian flag is the British Union Jack. The eight stripes of red, white, and blue represent both the U.S. flag and the eight major Hawai'ian islands. Designed about 1816 for King Kamehameha I of Hawai'i, the flag was adopted in 1959 when Hawai'i became the fiftieth state.

THE SEAL: In the middle of the seal is the state coat of arms, with King Kamehameha I on one side and the goddess of Liberty on the other. Around the two figures are taro and banana leaves, ferns, and a phoenix. The date, 1959, is the year that Hawai'i became a state and when the seal was adopted. At the bottom, the state motto, "The life of the land is perpetuated in righteousness," is written in Hawai'ian.

State Survey

Statehood: August 21, 1959

Origin of Name: According to legend, Hawai'i was named after a Polynesian chief, Hawai'i-loa, who led the Polynesian settlers to the Hawai'ian Islands. But legend also says that the name may have come from *Hawaiki*, the name of the Polynesian homeland to the west.

Nene

Nickname: Aloha State

Capital: Honolulu (on the island of O'ahu)

Bird: Nene, or Hawai'ian goose

Marine Mammal: Humpback whale

Flower: Yellow hibiscus

Tree: Kukui (candlenut tree)

Insect: Hawai'ian fly

Yellow hibiscus

HAWAI'I PONOI

"Hawai'i Ponoi," composed by King David Kalakaua, was proclaimed the national anthem of the Kingdom of Hawai'i in 1874. This beloved song continued to be sung after the United States annexed the islands, and in 1967 the state legislature passed an act making it the state song.

Words by H.M.King Kalakaua   **Music by H. Berger**

Ha - wai - i   po - no - i,   Na - na   i   kou - mo - i,
Ha - wai - i's   own true sons,   Be loy - al   to your chief

Ka - la - ni   A - li - i,   Ke   A - li - i.
Your coun - try's   leige and lord,   the   A - li - i.

Ma - ku - a   la - ni - e,   Ka - me - ha - me - ha e,
Fa - ther   a - bove   us all,   Ka - me - ha - me - ha e,

Na   ka - ua   e pa - le   Me   ka   i - he.
Who   guard-ed in the war   With   his   i - he.

GEOGRAPHY

Highest Point: 13,796 feet above sea level, at Mauna Kea

Lowest Point: Sea level along coast

Area: 6,459 square miles, including 36 square miles of inland water

Greatest Distance North to South (of the main islands): 230 miles

Greatest Distance East to West (of the main islands): 350 miles

Hottest Recorded Temperature: 100 degrees Fahrenheit in Puna, on the Big Island in 1931

Coldest Recorded Temperature: 12 degrees Fahrenheit on Mauna Kea in 1979

Average Annual Precipitation: 110 inches

Major Islands: Hawai'i (the Big Island), Kahoolawe, Kaua'i, Lana'i, Mau'i, Moloka'i, Ni'ihau, and O'ahu

Trees: Ash, banana, banyon, cedar, coconut, cypress, guava, juniper, kiawe, koa, kukui (candlenut), mango, noni, Norfolk pine, ohia, palm, papaya, redwood, sandalwood, sugi

Plants: Bamboo, fern, kaunaoa, olona, panini, pineapple, prickly pear cactus, sugarcane, taro, ti

Flowers: African violet, anthurium, carnation, frangipani, hibiscus, hydrangea, ilima, lantana, lobelia, lokelani, morning glory, orchid, passion flower, silversword

Fruits: Banana, breadfruit, coconut, guava, kiwi, kumquat, lime, lychee, mango, orange, papaya, passion fruit, pineapple, plum

Animals: Axis deer, cattle, chicken, coral, crab, dog, donkey, goat, Hawai'ian fly, hawksbill sea turtle, hoary bat, horse, lobster, mongoose, sheep, shrimp (prawns), snail, wild boar

Marine Mammals: Dolphin, monk seal, whale

Birds: Akepa, short-tailed albatross, amakihi, 'a'o, cardinal, coot, crow, duck, elepaio, finch, frigate, Hawai'ian honeycreeper, hawk, heron, 'I'iwi, millerbird, moorhen, myna, nene (Hawai'ian goose), noddy, owl, palila, parrotbill, peacock, petrel, plover, po'ouli, red-footed booby, shearwater, stilt, tern, thrush, white-tailed tropic bird

Fish: Ahi, a'u, barracuda, gray snapper, mahimahi (dolphin fish), marlin, ono, rectangular triggerfish, sailfish, shark, swordfish, tuna, ulua

Endangered Animals: Akaiapolau, Blackburn's sphinx moth, crested honeycreeper, Hawai'ian akepa, Hawai'ian common moorhen, Hawai'ian coot, Hawai'ian creeper, Hawai'ian crow, Hawai'ian dark-rumped petrel, Hawai'ian duck, Hawai'ian goose, Hawai'ian hawk, Hawai'ian hoary bat, Hawai'ian monk seal, Hawai'ian stilt, hawksbill sea turtle, humpback whale, Kaua'i akialoa, Kaua'i cave amphipod,

Kaua'i oo, Kaua'i akepa, large Kaua'i thrush, Laysan duck, Laysan finch, Mau'i akepa, Mau'i parrotbill, Moloka'i creeper, Moloka'i thrush, Nihoa finch, Nihoa millerbird, nukupu'u, O'ahu creeper, O'ahu elepaio, O'ahu tree snail, 'o'u, po'ouli, short-tailed albatross, small Kaua'i thrush

Endangered Plants and Areas: eke silversword, mixed sedge and grass montane bog, 'ohi'a forest, lama lowland dry forest

Oa'hu tree snail

TIMELINE

500 C.E. Polynesians from Pacific Islands arrive in Hawai'i.

c. 1200 Polynesians from Tahiti settle on Hawai'i and take over the islands.

1778 Captain James Cook reaches Hawai'i.

1795–1810 King Kamehameha I unites the Hawai'ian Islands.

1820 Protestant missionaries arrive in the islands.

1835 Hawai'i starts the first sugar plantation on Kaua'i.

1840 First written constitution grants powers to elected legislature.

1874 King Kalakaua restores Hawai'ian customs.

1875 Reciprocity treaty signed with the United States.

c. 1885 The Hawai'ian pineapple industry is founded.

1887 Hawai'ian League imposes "Bayonet Constitution" on King Kalakaua, which includes awarding the U.S. Navy exclusive use of Pearl Harbor as a port.

1891 Queen Lili'ukalani takes throne.

1893 A group of American and European businessmen and sugar planters, with American troops, overthrow Queen Lili'uokalani.

1894 Hawai'i becomes a republic; Sanford B. Dole, an American, becomes Hawai'i's first and only president.

1898 The United States annexes Hawai'i.

1900 Hawai'i becomes a U.S. territory; Hawai'ians become citizens of the United States.

1908 U.S. Congress authorizes the building of a naval base at Pearl Harbor.

1919 Jonah Kuhio Kalanianaole, Hawai'i's delegate to Congress, introduces first statehood bill.

1934 President Franklin D. Roosevelt is the first U.S. president to visit Hawai'i.

1941 The Japanese attack Pearl Harbor; the United States enters World War II.

1959 Hawai'i becomes the fiftieth state.

1992 Hurricane Iniki hits Hawai'i, causing eight deaths and $2 billion in damage.

1993 President Bill Clinton signs U.S. Public Law 103-150, which acknowledges that the overthrow of Queen Lili'uokalani and the Hawai'ian monarchy in 1893 by American and European businessmen and U.S. naval forces was illegal.

1994 Groups seeking Hawai'ian independence issue the Proclamation of Restoration of Independence of the Sovereign Nation State of Hawai'i.

1996 Last sugar plantation on the Big Island closes down.

2002 Hawai'i elects its first female governor, Linda Lingle.

2004 Record-breaking numbers of tourists (almost seven million) visit the Hawai'ian Islands.

2006 Kilauea, now continually flowing since 1983, creates the largest eruption of lava on the east rift zone in the past five hundred years.

ECONOMY

Agricultural Products: Avocados, bananas, beef, chicken, cocoa beans, coffee, corn, dairy products, eggs, fish, flowers, guavas, hogs, honey, macadamia nuts, papayas, passion fruit, pineapples, potatoes, prawns, sugarcane, taro

Manufactured Products: Chemicals, clothing, chocolate, concrete, food processing (including refined sugar, canned pineapple, and fruit juices), perfume, petroleum processing, printed materials

Pineapples

Natural Resources: Coral, crushed stone, pearls, sand, shells, titanium oxide (a paint pigment)

Business and Trade: Communications, including newspapers in many languages and radio and television stations; finance, insurance, and real estate; service industries, including the armed forces, hospitals, hotels, law firms, and rental-car agencies; tourism; transportation, including airlines, shipping, and trucking

CALENDAR OF CELEBRATIONS

Chinese New Year This festival comes in mid-January or February; visitors line the streets of Honolulu's Chinatown to watch the colorful lion dance in the Chinese New Year parade.

Narcissus Festival As part of the Chinese New Year celebrations, this festival on O'ahu runs for about five weeks and includes arts and crafts, food booths, and even a ball.

Ka Moloka'i Makahiki Every January, the island of Moloka'i holds a modern-day version of the classic makahiki festival. The day-long celebration begins with a traditional ceremony of chanting and dancing. It includes tournaments of Hawai'ian games and sports and ends with music, crafts, and Hawai'ian food.

Cherry Blossom Festival From late January until March, Honolulu hosts this Japanese festival that includes tea ceremonies, beautiful flowers, and ceremonial drummers.

Captain Cook Festival Captain James Cook is celebrated on Kaua'i every February with food, entertainment, and a footrace.

O'ahu Kite Festival This weekend event of colorful kite flying is held in early March at Kapiolani Park in Waikiki. Both professional and amateur kite fliers take part in the fun.

Prince Kuhio Day Every March 26 residents celebrate the birthday of Prince Jonas Kuhio, a Hawai'ian royal prince and Hawai'i's delegate to the U.S. Congress from 1903 to 1921. Celebrations are held on O'ahu and also on Kaua'i, the prince's birthplace.

Merrie Monarch Festival Beginning on Easter Sunday, in Hilo on the Big Island, this week-long festival celebrates King David Kalakaua, the Merrie Monarch, who brought back the hula to his people. Hawai'i's largest hula contest is the main attraction.

May Day May Day is Lei Day in Hawai'i; everyone celebrates this holiday on May 1 by wearing a lei. Lei-making contests are held on most of the islands.

Moloka'i Ka Hula Piko This festival on Moloka'i in mid-May celebrates the hula with dance performances and Hawai'ian food.

King Kamehameha Day All of Hawai'i celebrates the birthday of King Kamehameha I on June 11, a state holiday. Part of the traditional ceremony includes draping the statue of King Kamehameha with a beautiful 12-foot lei.

International Festival of the Pacific
This festival in mid-July in Hilo, on the Big Island, has a Pageant of Nations, with folk dances and costumes from Asia and the Pacific.

Prince Lot Hula Festival On O'ahu, the third Saturday in July, students from Hawai'i's most popular hula schools compete in hula contests.

Pan-Pacific Festival

Annual Ukulele Festival Ukulele music is celebrated in late July; hundreds of ukulele players come to Waikiki's Kapiolani Park Bandstand for this yearly event.

Obon Season This Japanese festival honoring ancestors is celebrated around the islands in July and August. The final event of the celebration is the famous floating lantern ceremony along Waikiki's Ala Wai Canal on the night of August 15.

Admission Day Held on the third Friday in August, this state holiday celebrates the day in 1959 when Hawai'i became a state. Hula and lei-making workshops are held on the Big Island.

Aloha Festivals For two months in September and October, the islands come alive with celebrations of Hawai'ian culture, including Hawai'ian sports, games, crafts, food, music, and dance.

Aloha Festival

Kona Coffee Cultural Festival Coffee is celebrated for ten days in Kailua-Kona, on the Big Island, the only place where coffee is grown in the United States. A parade in late October or early November and a coffee-picking contest are part of the entertainment.

STATE STARS

Daniel Kahikina Akaka (1934–   ) was born in Honolulu and became the first U.S. senator, in 1990, of Hawai'ian descent. Prior to becoming a senator, Akaka served in the U.S. House of Representatives from 1976 to 1990. As a child, Akaka was educated at the Kamehameha School for Boys. He is married to Mary Mildred Chong and is the grandfather of fourteen children. In 2005 Akaka was honored with Hawai'i's Out-standing Advocate for Children and Youth award. One of Senator Akaka's responsibilities in Congress is to serve on the Indian Affairs committee as well as the chair for the Congressional Task Force on Native Hawai'ian issues.

Heinrich (Henry) Berger (1844–1929) of Germany came to Hawai'i in 1872 to lead the Royal Hawai'ian Band. Berger led the band for forty-three years and became known as the father of Hawai'ian music for the songs he arranged for band performance. With King David Kalakaua he wrote "Hawai'i Ponoi," the national anthem, which later became Hawai'i's state song.

Hiram Bingham (1789–1869) became known for leading a group of Protestant missionaries to Hawai'i in 1820. With some of these mission-aries, Bingham created an alphabet for the Hawai'ian language and helped to translate the Bible into Hawai'ian. Bingham was the grandfather of Hiram Bingham (1875–1956), who was born in Honolulu and became an explorer in South America and discovered the Inca city of Machu Picchu, in the Andes Mountains of Peru. He later served as a U.S. senator from Connecticut.

Charles Reed Bishop (1822–1915) was born in New York, but became a banker in Hawai'i. Bishop gave a great deal of money to Hawai'i to improve its schools.

Bernice Pauahi Bishop (1831–1884) was a direct descendant of the Kamehameha royal family. She was born in Honolulu. At the age of nineteen she married, against the wishes of her family, Charles Reed Bishop, an American businessman. Her family had hoped she would marry one of the members of the Hawai'ian royalty. Before her death Bernice willed a large sum of money dedicated to the establishment of the Kamehameha School, whose mission was the education of orphans and children of Hawai'ian descent.

Benjamin J. Cayetano (1939–   ) was the first Filipino American to hold office in the United States. As governor of Hawai'i (from 1994 to 2002), Cayetano was known for his support of Hawai'i's tourist industry.

James Cook (1728–1779), an English explorer, was the first European to set foot on Hawai'i. Cook was a captain in the British navy when, in 1778, he landed in the Hawai'ian Islands. He called them the Sandwich Islands, after his sponsor, the Earl of Sandwich. A year later, on a return voyage, Cook was killed by a group of Hawai'ians who were angry at his harsh treatment of them.

James D. Dole (1877–1958) was the son of Sanford B. Dole, president of the Republic of Hawai'i. In 1922 James Dole set up a 15,000-acre pineapple plantation on Lana'i, which is sometimes called Pineapple Island. Dole is recognized for having established the pineapple industry in Hawai'i.

Sanford B. Dole (1844–1926) was the first and only president of the Republic of Hawai'i. In 1893 Dole led a small group of businessmen who removed Queen Liliuokalani from the throne. A year later he became Hawai'i's president. Dole also served as the first governor of the territory of Hawai'i.

Don Ho (1930–) has done more than anyone else to keep Hawai'ian music alive. Ho is the best-known Hawai'ian entertainer. His shows for tourists in Hawai'i, especially in Honolulu, and his countless appearances on television programs have made him popular throughout the United States.

Daniel Inouye (1924–), born in Honolulu, is the first Japanese American to serve in the U.S. Congress. During his long career Inouye has served in the Hawai'ian State House of Representatives and the Hawai'ian Senate. In 1959 he became Hawai'i's first U.S. representative to Congress. Later, he was elected to the Senate. Inouye gained national fame by serving on the committee that investigated the Watergate scandals of President Richard M. Nixon's administration.

Daniel Inouye

Duke Kahanamoku (1890–1968), the famous Hawai'ian surfer, was known as the human fish for his achievements in surfing, swimming, and water polo. A gold medal-winning swimmer in the 1912, 1920, and 1924 Olympics, Duke also played on the Olympic water polo team in 1932 at the age of forty-two. Although a gifted swimmer, Duke is best known for his surfing tricks, such as riding backward and doing handstands on his flying board, maneuvers that earned him the title "the father of modern surfing." He also served as sheriff of Honolulu for twenty-nine years.

David Kalakaua (1836–1891), known as the Merrie Monarch, was king of Hawai'i from 1874 to 1891. With his wife, Queen Kapiolani, Kalakaua encouraged his people to keep Hawai'ian customs alive. King Kalakaua's "merry" deeds included bringing back Hawai'ian music and the hula, long repressed by the missionaries. With Heinrich Berger he wrote "Hawai'i Ponoi," the Hawai'ian national anthem, which later became the state song.

Emma Kaleleonalani (1836–1885) was the daughter of George Nae'a and Fanny Kekelaokalani Young. In 1856 Emma married King Kamehameha IV. She was known as a humanitarian queen who looked out for her people. Queen Emma, along with her husband, were dedicated to saving the native Hawai'ian population that was fast declining in her lifetime. Toward this effort, she helped to finance the construction of a hospital. Upon her death, Emma left the bulk of her estate in trust for the hospital in Honolulu that is called Queen's Hospital, which later was renamed Queen's Medical Center.

Emma Kaleleonalani

Kamehameha I (1758?–1819), also known as Kamehameha the Great, was the founder of the kingdom of Hawai'i. Kamehameha I was king when Captain Cook landed in Hawai'i in 1778. By 1810 he had conquered all the Hawai'ian Islands. The son of a chief, he took the name Kamehameha, meaning "the one set apart."

Kamehameha II (1797–1824) ruled Hawai'i from 1819 to 1824. Although he was a son of Kamehameha I (the Great), he did not agree with the feudal, social, and religious restrictions of the ancient kapu system. During his reign the ancient kapu system of taboos was eliminated. He died of measles while visiting King George IV of England.

Kamehameha III (1813–1854) was a son of Kamehameha I (the Great) and a younger brother of Kamehameha II. At the age of twelve, upon the death of Kamehameha II, he ascended the throne of Hawai'i, ruling until 1854. In 1840 he set up the first Hawai'ian constitution, which later gave Hawai'ians the right to vote, to own land, and to share power with the king.

Kamehameha IV (1834–1863), also known as Alexander Liholiho, was king of Hawai'i from 1854 to 1863. He was the grandson of Kamehameha I (the Great) and the nephew and adopted son of Kamehameha III. During his reign Hawai'ians were dying from infectious illnesses brought to the islands by visitors from Europe. As a result, Kamehameha IV, with Queen Emma, built the Queen's Hospital in Honolulu to care for sick people. After his only child died in 1862, he left the throne.

Kamehameha V (1830–1872), also known as Lot Kamehameha, was the last of the Kamehameha kings. An older brother of Kamehameha IV, he ruled Hawai'i from 1863 to 1872. During his reign a new constitution was approved by Hawai'ians and sugarcane became an important crop. The king died on his forty-second birthday, December 11. He never married and had no heir to the throne. David Kalakaua became king upon his death.

Lydia Lili'uokalani (1838–1917) was the last of the Hawai'ian kings and queens. After her brother, King David Kalakaua, died, Lili'uokalani tried to bring back power to the Hawai'ian throne. But American settlers and investors who owned most of Hawai''i's resources overthrew and humiliated her in a sort of house arrest, and Hawai'i became a republic. The queen, who ruled only two years, from 1891 to 1893, is remembered for her song, "Aloha 'Oe," which became Hawai'i's song of farewell.

Bette Midler

Bette Midler (1945–   ), born in Honolulu, is one of the best-known female entertainers in the United States. Midler's forceful singing style and talented acting in such films as *The Stepford Wives* (2004) have made her an international celebrity.

Ellison Shoji Onizuka (1946–1986), the first Hawai'ian astronaut, was one of the seven people to die in the explosion aboard the space shuttle *Challenger* in 1986. A hero to people across the nation, Onizuka became the first Japanese American to make a flight into space. During his trip aboard the space shuttle *Discovery* in 1985, Onizuka realized the risks of space flight. After the voyage he told reporters, "You're really aware that you're on top of a monster; you're totally at the mercy of the vehicle."

Ellison Shoji Onizuka

Cathy Song (1955–   ), a native of Honolulu of Chinese and Korean descent, is one of the most popular young poets in the United States. Song's three books of poetry, *Picture Bride* (1983), *Frameless Windows, Squares of Light* (1988), and *School Figures* (1994) are filled with beautiful visual images and memories of her childhood. As a poet and a creative-writing teacher at the University of Hawai'i at Manoa, Song stresses the importance of writing about cultural heritage and personal experiences.

John L. Stevens (1820–1895) was a U.S. envoy (diplomat) to Hawai'i from 1889 to 1893. Stevens played a large part in the 1893 rebellion that removed Queen Lili'uokalani from the throne. He was also involved in setting up the new government under Sanford B. Dole.

Kathleen Tyau (1946–   ) has done much in her writing to depict the Hawai'ian way of life. A native of O'ahu, Tyau's funny novel *A Little Too Much Is Enough* describes Hawai'ian delights, from making poi to eating a nine-course wedding feast. Her second book, *Makai* (1999) is a novel about women's experiences in Hawai'i during World War II.

John Waihee (1946–   ), born in Honoka'a, is the state's first governor of Hawai'ian descent. During his term, from 1986 to 1994, Hawai'i became the first state to adopt universal health care. Waihee also took a strong stand on protecting Hawai'i's fragile environment.

TOUR THE STATE

O'AHU

Waikiki Beach (Honolulu) This busy beach is ringed with high-rise hotels, beautiful orange sunsets, swimmers, surfers, and plenty of tourists.

Kapiolani Park (Honolulu) King Kalakaua gave this 200-acre park to the people of Honolulu in 1877. Situated below Diamond Head at the end of Waikiki, the park has an aquarium, a zoo, hula show grounds, a bandstand, tennis courts, and space for kite flying. It is the largest and oldest park in Hawai'i and was named after Queen Kapiolani.

I'olani Palace (Honolulu) Once the home of Hawai'ian monarchy, this is the only royal palace in the United States. Today, the palace offers guided tours through its throne room, palace grounds, and museum.

Kamehameha Statue (Honolulu) The statue of Kamehameha I (the Great) stands opposite I'olani Palace and is a popular tourist spot. It is especially popular on June 11, the king's birthday, when people affectionately dress the statue in a long lei.

USS *Arizona* Memorial (Pearl Harbor) Visitors can see the remains of the American battleship *Arizona*, which was sunk when the U.S. ships in Pearl Harbor were attacked by the Japanese on December 7, 1941.

Diamond Head (Southeast O'ahu) This 760-foot-high extinct volcano crater was named by British sailors who thought that the sparkling crystals on top of the volcano were diamonds. A hiking trail to the top of Diamond Head offers a great view of the island.

USS Arizona *Memorial*

Sea Life Park (Southeast O'ahu) Fish, sea turtles, eels, hammerhead
sharks, Hawai'ian monk seals, and performing dolphins and whales
can be seen at this marine park.

Polynesian Cultural Center (Laie) This reconstruction of villages
from Samoa, New Zealand, Fiji, Tahiti, Tonga, the Marquesas, and
Hawai'i features huts, weavings, tapa cloth, crafts, and Polynesian
dances and games.

Dole Pineapple Plantation (Wahiawa) Pineapple fields, a pineapple processing plant, and a free cup of refreshing pineapple juice make this a popular place to visit.

HAWAI'I—THE BIG ISLAND

Kealakekua Bay (South Kona) A monument marks the place where Captain James Cook was killed on February 14, 1779.

Puako Petroglyphs (north of Kona) Here can be seen one of the largest and oldest collections of petroglyphs (carvings on stone of humans, animals, objects, and shapes) found in Hawai'i.

Parker Ranch (Waimea) Visitors to this huge ranch can tour two historic homes and a museum. They have a wealth of paintings, photographs, quilts, old saddles, and surfboards.

Hawai'i Tropical Botanical Garden (Hamakua Coast) Thousands of tropical plants, lush streams and waterfalls, and a lily pond make this garden in a rain forest a beautiful serene place to visit.

King Kamehameha Birthplace Located out of the way at the northern tip of the island, the place that King Kamehameha I was born sits next to one of the oldest *heiau's* (ancient temples) in the islands.

Hapuna Beach This is the only long white sand beach on the Big Island. It is located along the Kohala shoreline on the west side of the island.

Hawai'i Volcanoes National Park (near Pahala) This unique national park has two active volcanoes, lava flows, a desert, and beautiful beaches.

Hawai'i Volcanoes National Park

MAU'I

Lahaina (western Mau'i) Once the royal court of Mau'i chiefs and whaling town, Lahaina has some of the best sightseeing spots in Hawai'i, including the Pioneer Inn, the whaling museum, and the old mission.

'Iao Valley State Park (Wailuku area) Iao Needle rises more than 1,000 feet into the air and is a treat for amateur photographers visiting this state park.

Haleakala National Park (Haleakala) Haleakala Crater is the main site in this amazing national park, named for Haleakala, a large active volcano. Spectacular sunrises at the rim of the crater earn Haleakala its name, House of the Sun.

MOLOKA'I

Palaau State Park (Central Moloka'i) A five-minute walk from the parking lot, Kalaupapa Overlook is the dramatic attraction in this state park. This 1,600-foot cliff offers an aerial view of Kalaupapa Peninsula without the airplane!

Waikolu Lookout (Central Moloka'i) At 3,600 feet, this lookout point gives visitors an awesome view of Waikolu Valley and the ocean beyond.

Kamakou Preserve (Central Moloka'i) Just beyond Waikolu Lookout is Kamakou Preserve, a rain forest where many rare and endangered plants and animals can be found.

Mauna Loa (West End) This mountain range lives up to its name, which means Long Mountain. Its highest point is Puunana, at 1,381 feet.

LANA'I

Lana'i City (Central Lana'i) This once-bustling plantation town still has some pineapple fields, tin-roofed houses, brightly painted buildings, lush yellow flowers, and Dole Park, which is lined with tall Norfolk and Cook Island pines.

Munro Trail (Northwest Lana'i) A visitor can walk this 8.5-mile dirt road in a day and can view most of the Hawai'ian Islands from various points along the route.

KAUA'I

Menehune Fish Pond (East Side) The misty Haupu Ridge in the background and the stone wall that is said to have been built by the menehunes (the "little people" of Hawai'ian myth) make this fish pond a mysterious place to visit.

Wailua Falls (East Side) A scenic 80-foot waterfall.

Wailua Falls

Fern Grotto (East Side) The riverboat tour up the Wailua River to the Fern Grotto, a cave beneath a fern-covered rock face, is Kaua'i's busiest and most romantic tourist attraction.

Kilauea Point National Wildlife Refuge (North Shore) This wildlife refuge, surrounding an old lighthouse, looks just like a picture postcard.

Koloa (South Shore) Hawai'i's first sugar plantation was started in Koloa in 1835. Sugarcane fields, sugar exhibits, and the old cane worker's town make interesting sights.

Waimea Canyon (West Side) This spectacular canyon, which is nick-named the Grand Canyon of the Pacific, earns its name with a colorful river-cut gorge, beautiful waterfalls, and deep-red earth.

FUN FACTS

Hawai'i is the southernmost state in the Union.

The fiftieth star, representing Hawai'i, was added to the U.S. flag on July 4, 1960.

Hawai'i is one of the few states that does not change its clocks for daylight savings time in the spring and fall. Also, Hawai'i has its own time zone: Hawai'ian Standard Time.

The *pulelehua*, or Kamehameha butterfly, is one of the only two butterflies that are native to Hawai'i.

A star called Arcturus (or *Hokule'a* in Hawai'ian) rises directly over Honolulu and was used by ancient mariners to locate the present day Hawai'ian Islands.

The movie *Jurassic Park* (1993) was filmed on O'ahu and Kaua'i. The movie *Waterworld* (1995) was filmed off the Big Island's western shores.

Find Out More

If you would like to learn more about Hawai'i, check your library, bookstore, or video store for these titles:

STATE BOOKS

Johnston, Joyce. *Hawaii* (2nd edition). Minneapolis: Lerner, 2001.

Potter, Norris W., Lawrence M. Kasdon, and Ann Rayson. *History of the Hawaiian Kingdom.* Honolulu: Bess Press, 2003.

SPECIAL INTEREST BOOKS

Hoover, John P. *Hanauma Bay: A Marine Guide to Hawaii's Most Popular Nature Preserve.* Honolulu: Mutual Publishing, 2002.

Kalman, Bobby. *Endangered Monk Seals.* New York: Crabtree Publishing, 2004.

Middleton, Susan, and David Littschwager. *Remains of a Rainbow: Rare Plants and Animals of Hawaii.* Washington, D.C.: National Geographic, 2003.

DVD

American Aloha: Hula Beyond Hawaii. 55 minutes. Custom Flix, 2003.

Hawaii Islands Video Postcard. 90 minutes. Crevier Enterprises, 2005.

Hawaii Songs of Aloha. 77 minutes. Mountain Apple, 2000.

WEB SITES

Hawai'i State Government

http://www.hawaii.gov

Find out what Hawai'i's government is working on, check out school news, discover who the state and federal senators are, or learn about interesting things to do in the islands at this Web site.

Hawai'i Kids

http://www.hawaiischoolreports.com/culture/kids.htm

Read Hawai'ian myths or learn more about Hawai'i's volcanoes. These are just some of the things you can do at this site, which is rich in details about life in Hawai'i.

USS *Arizona* Memorial

http://www.nps.gov/usar/home.htm

Discover the history behind the USS *Arizona* Memorial, as well as the events surrounding the attack on Pearl Harbor on December 7, 1941.

Index

Page numbers in **boldface** are illustrations and charts.

ABOUT THE AUTHORS

Jake Goldberg is a writer and editor who lives in New York City. He has written biographies for young readers, as well as several books on food and agriculture. He has traveled widely in Europe and Asia, and in the Americas his journeys have taken him from the Hawai'ian Islands to the Inuit villages of the Arctic to the Andes and the upper Amazon basin.

Joyce Hart lived for many years in Hilo and in Hawai'i, on the Big Island. She has seen Mauna Loa erupt and has watched the hot red lava flow down the sides of Kilauea in the middle of the night. While some of her friends shivered through cold winters on the American mainland, she floated on the warm waters of Hapuna Beach, while staring up in wonder at the snow on top of Mauna Kea. She has also learned much about the Aloha spirit from the people of North Kohala. *Mahalo.*